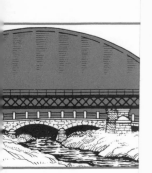

"L'aube de L'Islam"

River

Baptiste

Pavillon

Risso

avenue

Boulevard

Place
Garibaldi

rue

Barla

Route followed by the gang from
the entrance via the river,
under the Palais des Expositions,
to the Société Générale bank.

FRIC-FRAC

The Great
Riviera Bank Robbery

Books by Albert Spaggiari

Faut pas rire avec les barbares
Fric-Frac: The Great Riviera Bank Robbery

FRIC-FRAC

*The Great
Riviera Bank Robbery*

ALBERT SPAGGIARI

Translated from the French
by Martin Sokolinsky

*ILLUSTRATED WITH PHOTOGRAPHS
AND MAPS*

Houghton Mifflin Company Boston   1979

4-26-90

First published in French, under the title *Les égouts du paradis,* by Éditions Albin
Michel. Copyright © 1978 by Éditions Albin Michel and Pierre-Marcel Favre,
Publi SA.

Library of Congress Cataloging in Publication Data

Spaggiari, Albert.
  Fric-frac: the great Riviera bank robbery.
  Translation of Les égouts du paradis.
  1. Spaggiari, Albert. 2. Crime and criminals—
France—Biography. 3. Bank robberies—France—Nice.
I. Title.
HV6248.S6139A413   346.1'55   [B]   79–416
ISBN 0–395–27764–7

Printed in the United States of America

V 10 9 8 7 6 5 4 3 2 1

Foreword

EACH WEEK, EACH DAY, I've been getting myself ready for the jump from the third-story window of the court building. Between times, I've been writing this book. I know that once I'm on the outside, I'll never have a chance to do it.

So I'm writing and waiting. That friend should have been here three weeks ago, but he hasn't come.

Yes, my friend should have been here.

Years ago, we took an oath to help each other. I can still hear him telling me, "If you're ever in jail, nothing will stop me. You have my word on that." It doesn't matter whether he owed me something or simply wanted me to do the same for him someday. Of that whole pack of bums that I hung around with, he was the only one who could be counted on to keep his word.

I remember those days, our wild ideas, our eagerness . . .

I've got plenty of time now . . . time to think over the years that have flown by. Now there's nothing left of the hero of the old days, nothing but a two-hundred-pound carcass in the clink and a pair of stooped shoulders.

But doing time in jail isn't all that bad. What bothers me is the fact that I'm not getting any younger. I still have so many things to do.

I know what it's like to be on the outside. First of all, there are my pals. We're glad to get together, we talk, we have a few drinks, and we forget. That's the way it goes.

But I haven't forgotten anything, friend. Nothing.

I don't know what's going to happen in the next few hours, in the next few days. I only know — and you must know this, too — that every Thursday I go to see the judge. And that one of these Thursdays (I still don't know which one) I'm going to jump right out one of those windows in his chamber. I'll make that jump because either you'll have come, friend, or I'll have gotten fed up with waiting.

There's a good chance that this book — if it does ever get published — will appear after my death.

My dedication is simply: amen.

Contents

16 pages of photographs follow page 120

PART ONE

PREPARATIONS

CHAPTER 1

Don't Try to . . .

MY NAME IS Albert Spaggiari. As I've already told you, I'm in prison. My cell is located on the ground floor. It's about two yards wide and three yards long. I keep training for the jump: opening an imaginary window (the one that's in the judge's chamber) with a quick move. Then I get up on my bunk to practice keeping my feet close together when jumping.

Who knows what tomorrow holds in store for me? A few weeks ago, I made headlines all over the world. And just a month ago, every cop on earth had my photo in his pocket. I'm the brain behind the bank heist in Nice.

The newspapers mentioned sixty million francs — maybe even a hundred million. I don't know too much about that. The papers know.

That's the way I am. I've always been broke, for the simple reason that money doesn't mean anything to me. I guess that makes you laugh. Well, go ahead — you've got plenty of laughs coming.

Actually, I think you'd be wasting your time to try to classify me. It could be a complicated business, trying to get me to fit some IBM card. Unless, of course, you feel like short-circuiting a computer. In that case, you've come to the right party.

In the old days, I attached some importance to what people thought about me. But I finally realized that most people just don't think, *period.* The years went by, and today I don't give a damn about people and what they think. Go ahead and make me into some kind of statistic, for all I care.

The police files, indictments, and records bearing my name mean no more to me than a bunch of old candy wrappers. Some bright people say that when a traveler faces the south, he's got his back to the north. They claim that it's practically inevitable. Well, those guys are trying to put one over on you. Anybody who schedules his trips isn't a traveler — he's a sailor. I say that because I'm a voyager. A voyager without compass or chart. I travel and I dream. I've spent my life dreaming. For me, a dream is the reality you have just before the big problems start.

As you can see for yourself, the only thing that I have in common with the average citizen is a certain genetic similarity. That's something that bothers a lot of people. But maybe I get a kick out of bothering them.

Why am I writing this book? Because I volunteered to tell the story to the cops — without going beyond that. So you might as well read it, too, if you're so inclined. What's more, people have made up too many cockeyed stories about me. (Some of them make me out to be almost superhuman.) But that isn't what makes me see red. Before some writer who's hard up for a story decides to concoct my biography, I'd better write it myself. That's only logical.

Albert Spaggiari, alias Bert. Soldier of fortune, political activist, thief, jailbird . . . I have my humble side and my megalomaniac side. Basically, however, I stay in the middle of the road.

If you want more information, let me say that I was born under the sign of Sagittarius. My blood type is B. The shape of my head is dolichocephalic. I have some friends in the right places.

I like women. All kinds of women — especially brunettes, blondes, and redheads. I'm also fond of animals. All kinds of animals, but mostly the ones that are hunted, because we share the same fate.

Like everyone else, I have my roots. It's something that's always surprised me. If they'd told me, "You weren't born like everybody else, Bert; you were found," I would have believed them. According to what I heard, my great-grandfather on my mother's side packed his bags on his eightieth birthday to go squander his life savings at the roulette tables of Monte-Carlo. His son, my mother's father, a lucky fellow who owned property and could retire at thirty, was said to have gone off with a bundle of clothes over a stick, abandoning wife and kids, ending up a hobo.

On my father's side, things were just as colorful. One day, a band of seven roughnecks crossed over from Italy into France along the Durance River. They managed all right, swinging crowbars and ax handles when they had to. Wars and miscellaneous accidents scattered them afterward. I'm the only one left to carry on the family name.

A bean pole that can run like the wind. My ancestors were roughnecks and tramps in Provence. At the outset, that was the one thing I had going for me.

I was haled into court and sentenced a thousand times. I was innocent. When a guy is sincere, he's always innocent.

"Spaggiari, you're daydreaming! Just for that, you'll write, 'I must not daydream', one hundred times."

"Spaggiari, subtract eight from fifteen!"

"Spaggiari, solitary confinement!"

"Spaggiari, five years at hard labor!"

"Stripped of your rank . . . Forbidden to reside in this territory . . ."

Finally, the little wop got sore. He was fed up. He'd seen too much, heard too much. It was you, the draft evaders, the profiteers in piastres and blood, who ruined me. You shouldn't have isolated me from the mercenaries, where I belonged. I was fighting for a set of ideals, you cocksuckers! All you people ever wanted out of that war was to line your own pockets. But we were there because we loved the danger and the camaraderie.

Albert Spaggiari won't go around complaining anymore. You kept telling him over and over that he had to keep his mouth shut, that he was just a parasite. It's only natural that he wound up believing it. He turned into a loner, outside your system for good.

I believe that any criminal act against society is a political action. Most of all, robbery. But I don't mean petty theft, which usually involves picking the pockets of poor people. I mean Robbery. Now that's an art you've got to be born with. It also represents man's greatest hope of attaining his goal by his own means. Any other way is like betting on horses or buying lottery tickets.

Go ahead, look shocked, you hypocrites! Everybody steals. The scope of that stealing ranges from daily pilferage (chicken feed) to organized, official fraud. In terms of the skills involved, from apprentice to master craftsman.

I'm a robber. It's because I'm honest that I tell you. Well, as a great Finnish poet used to say, "That's not everything."

For eight years prior to this adventure — this heist, if you prefer — I'd been in a stupor. Business. I tried that, too. I tried everything. I ran a photo store. For eight years I stayed in a kind of coma. Income, value-added tax, deductions, social security, insurance, local taxes, enlargements, borders, highways, parking lots, tickets, contributions, the sanitation department, signs, street cleaners, television, discounts, bribery, favoritism, cops, hospitals, parish feasts, membership dues, group insurance . . . I paid for everything. For the children I didn't have, for world idiocy. They even made me pay for my own shit, which was actually fertilizing the soil. The tax collectors and parasites paraded into my shop, rushed at me, cornered me. I don't understand it at all. Up to that point, my only stock in trade had been my own life. People got me all mixed up; they were pushing me around. And I had to watch my step — otherwise, I was in trouble.

"If you don't know — ten percent increase."

"If you don't smile — ten percent increase."

Pay, you stupid son of a bitch. Cough up! Crawl!

Eight years . . . Eight damned years of that.

At first, that photo store had represented an opportunity to get out of political activism, without retaliation. I was fed up with hearing the same interchangeable speeches, fed up with punching the same people, with begging, with putting up posters, with waiting, with saying, "Yes, but . . ."

I'd picked the wrong dream once more. What a mess!

Yet, at the start, I couldn't really complain. Lots of companies gave me credit, whether they liked it or not. Audi, my wife, did the work of three people. What was more, I didn't have expensive tastes. I spent next to nothing on clothes. I ate at home every day. I spent my holidays with the family. As for my car, it was a Land Rover, built to last forever.

Oh, sure, we treated ourselves to a trip now and then, to keep from going crazy. The Sahara — do you remember that, Audi, darling? The Sahara, where I dreamed that we'd live someday, without chains and without roof.

Do you remember Arlit, darling? They've discovered uranium there. Do you remember Iferouane? Iferouane at the end of the Aire River. They built a housing project there. There's a policeman and a little station house.

Do you remember R'guiba, that old French sergeant we met on the *piste* at Bir Moghreim? He was hunting in order to feed a village that was starving.

But those trips couldn't wash away the bitter taste of the wasted years. Much to the contrary. With each passing year, I got deeper into debt. The inescapable failure of my life was there, at the bottom of my drinks, my beds, my suppers. Me, Spaggiari, adventurer, I had set myself up as a pimp with a five-yard stretch of sidewalk in front of a camera store.

Oh, sure, I still had The Wild Geese, my place in the country. My hermitage in the Bézaudun Forest, in the high country back of Nice. It was an old shepherd's cottage that I'd converted. I began going there instead of to the apartment we'd rented over the store. But even those triumphant mornings at Bézaudun; even the beauty of your eyes, darling; even my hundred-year-old oaks, my mountain, and my dogs, couldn't drive away the shame of being a pimp. The shame of growing old, of coughing up my money for state-administered whoring. The shame of breaking my vows, of not being on the go anymore, of having to cover my face so that I couldn't see old dreams fallen by the wayside.

And then, one fine day, a pal landed in Nice. His sudden visit would turn my life upside down. His name was Claude, but I used to call him "Sixty-eight," in honor of May 1968.

May 1968 — do you remember? The Algerian War. Vets sat in their wheelchairs; the ones who'd done Indo-China pushed. The last survivors of the OAS* were busy fighting for anybody

---

*Translator's note: the Organisation Armée Secrète, made up of disaffected French army officers and their men, who wanted France to retain Algeria as a colony.

who paid enough. Arpint Pont, cut to pieces by the Viets, was turned over to the Americans. Thierry got himself eaten alive by blacks in the Congo. Zoffner was dismembered when his car exploded in Argentina. Fighting with the Kurds, Pépin caught a bullet in the head. André Perez was an instructor with the Green Berets, and Carco taught counterinsurgency to the children of the Boers.

The more desperate ones had committed suicide, like Michel Garcia, by blowing their brains out; or Cassou, by an overdose. There were also unexplained, mysterious deaths, like Ruiz' or Lods'.

The wisest ones had switched to Coca-Cola. The more adventurous were treasure-hunting in the West Indies. The craziest stuck up banks and wound up in jail. I was just back from somewhere or other, basking in the Nice sun, looking up old pals and taking stock of broken dreams. That was when May '68 struck like a summer storm.

Jesus, I jumped on the bandwagon. In no time, I was in Paris. I phoned everybody. I went running all over the city, frantically trying to call out the old guard. But, once again, those imbeciles failed to see the light and ran away. It would have been the chance of a lifetime to screw the commies and their legal mafia, the CGT.*

I was right there, in the middle of things. I even managed to get into the fighting. Out of habit. Just for laughs. I knew it was a hopeless battle, but I couldn't help wading in.

I couldn't help it because I'm a wolf. I was raised like a wolf and I've lived like one. Being a wolf is my natural instinct, my first reflex. I got fed up with all those Communists and their cry-baby demonstrations. Marchais and his clique had cas-

*Translator's note: the Confédération Générale de Travail, the French trade union federation, mostly communist since 1947.

trated regiments of sheep by promising them refrigerators and electric blankets. And it worked! Dopy France! These lunatics talk about justice and social equality for a better life. What a crock of shit! They just anesthetize you with paid vacations; make you into faggots, without pride, without backbone, degraded by the certainty of having enough to eat as long as you talk loud enough to drive everybody crazy. What shit! Comrades, keep your sheep! I prefer the big slobs on the right — at least they show their colors.

I'd made the trip to Paris for nothing, so I decided to join in the fun. One night I got myself trapped in a fierce riot. I had to beat a retreat. As we fled wildly, I heard somebody yelling behind us, "Number Thirty-one, Boule' Mich' . . . there's a courtyard. . . the wall isn't very high."

I took a chance and made a dash for the carriage door. The CRS* gave us a run for our money that night. The guy who'd tipped me off about the courtyard must have been right behind me. I went diving into the doorway, then raced through the archway and into the courtyard. There it was! To the right of an outbuilding stood a wall only three and a half feet high.

"Let's go!" I yelled, hauling myself over the top.

In an instant, I was straddling the wall, ready to . . . Damn it! I was alone. I'd lost my guide.

What are you supposed to do when you meet a brother in a battle and then you lose him? You don't stop to think. You do an about-face and go straight back into the fight.

There I was, on the streets again. The riot was at a fever pitch. Helmeted CRS were beating the crap out of the demonstrators who couldn't get away. Billy clubs rained down from every side. Christ, I went back into the doorway of Number 31.

---

*Translator's note: Compagnies Républicaines de Sécurité, the militarized police.

Quick, the trash cans. I turned one over, then another. In the third, there were bottles. I took one in each hand.

Now most of the guardsmen were clubbing in the opposite direction. About a hundred yards to my right, two CRS were dragging a demonstrator toward the trucks. It had to be my brother.

I smashed one bottle against the first cop's knee. The second cop, who held his rifle in one hand while gripping the wounded demonstrator's shoulder with the other, didn't have time to lower his visor when a bottle broke over his skull. But he did manage to give me a butt stroke in the chest. My knees buckled. There I was, on all fours, gasping for breath. I was down for the count. So were the two CRS. That was all I needed: a whole squad came double-timing my way. I grabbed my buddy by the belt, carrying him, half-dragging him. Though dazed, I knew that if the guardsmen caught up with me, they would bash my skull in. I don't know how I made it to Number 31. The last few yards were terrible. With one mighty heave, the last bit of strength in my body, I threw the kid into the shelter of the carriage gateway. Then I blacked out. It was a good thing, too. If I hadn't fallen, I would have received a rifle butt over my head. But then I was on all fours again. Instinctively, I kicked out backward at the CRS and caught him on the hip. The kick wasn't all that powerful, but it threw him off balance long enough for me to dive into the carriage gateway. I slammed the heavy wooden door and braced myself against it. An instant later they began smashing their rifle butts against the door. That hammering rang in my ears. I knew I couldn't hold out for long.

Then all of a sudden — nothing. I waited. It must be a trick, I thought, or a battering ram will splinter the oak and knock me senseless. Still nothing. I kept my ear cocked. The tenants of the building were dumping buckets of water out the windows. "Gestapo! This is private property," they yelled. "Are you supposed to be protecting property or destroying it? We pay taxes, and that's what you do?"

The whistle shrilled over the hubbub.

"Sections two and three, fall in at the trucks," barked a voice over a bullhorn.

Hurried footsteps rang out against the pavement, then moved away.

Half an hour later, two volunteers helped me to move the wounded fellow up to Katie's apartment. I was living with Katie. Afterward, I called for a doctor.

Katie was a nice girl. Really built, but her taste in clothes was something else. She could be a pain in the neck at times. All in all, though, we got along nicely. Katie lived in a garret, and rafters took up most of the room in her apartment. To get to the kitchen, you practically had to crawl. I remember that the place had a nice smell of pepper and licorice. Aside from the two beds, all the furniture was made of crates and boards. I have pleasant memories of that garret and those days.

A week went by before Sixty-eight, or Claude, was up on his feet again. Outside, the clamor of the revolt was dying. The everyday world had regained the upper hand. The revolt was finished. The students and the workers threw in the towel, and the heroes of World War II paraded down the Champs-Elysées. And in the course of conversation I learned that my Sixty-eight, my Claude, hadn't been the one who'd tipped me off to the hiding place at Number 31. I'd gotten my man mixed up and had dragged in some other *mec.* It didn't make any difference, though; this one was a nice guy. He was full of piss and vinegar. Plenty worried, too, because they'd snapped his picture just as he was heaving a Molotov cocktail. Forever making mountains out of molehills, he imagined that the police wanted him for murder. I told him that he could come along to Nice with me. He turned down my offer because he couldn't believe that the revolution was over. He had started a riot with striking workers at a factory outside Paris. So, full of confidence, he went back there one morning. He returned around noon, wearing a dejected look. I didn't ask him anything about it.

He said, "If the offer still stands, I'm ready to go down to Nice."

Later, he told me that the workers hadn't recognized him or, because of his long hair, had pretended not to know him. They'd wanted nothing to do with him. He'd persisted, and they'd actually come to blows.

Afterward, there were the elections in Nice. I got him a two-month job pasting up posters for a wealthy man who was paying in advance for his defeat.

Then, one Monday morning Sixty-eight went off, dancing in the footsteps of Alexander the Great. Eight years later, a wolf showed up at my door, without a word of warning. It was Sixty-eight. He'd changed quite a bit. Yes, indeed, he certainly had changed. And so had I.

He'd caught a slug in the shoulder and had received shrapnel wounds in the belly on the Iraqi border, where getting contraband across was becoming increasingly difficult. Only two of the fourteen smugglers had come out alive. He'd been forced to change hemispheres. En route for Caracas, he had stopped in Nice only for two days. I was barely hanging on to my sanity, and his visit really blew my mind. It wasn't the things that he told me, but the fact that so many years had gone by. And then it was his expression. The way he looked when he lifted his eyes toward my sign, PHOTO LA VALLIÈRE, when he ran his gaze over the store. And when he watched through the window as the bus stopped to pick up two passengers, then sped away on the Route de Marseille.

Afterward, we went to the little café across the street for a drink. Sometimes it doesn't take much to get things going. It all happens so fast. One day, on your way back from the toilet, you catch a glimpse of yourself in an old bistro mirror. Suddenly, you realize that the years have slipped away. Aside from your face, nothing seems changed. And you go back to the little green coffee cup, standing on the zinc counter; you go back to your friend. A guy who is just passing through, whose life is full of adventure while you're in a rut. And it tears you in half.

I think it happened right then and there, when I was standing in front of the zinc bar. The idea for the heist of the century dawned on me.

The next evening, while taking Sixty-eight to the airport, I asked him to let me have his address. I said that I might be needing him for a job that would be worth his while. He gave me his address.

Things really began happening after that.

CHAPTER 2

A Plan That Was Something Special

UNFORTUNATELY, time erases sound as well as silence. I've never wanted to talk about my friend Plantier, a teller in a branch of the Société Générale. A pensioned police officer, he'd somehow managed to shed all the stupidity that's associated with that occupation. From his career as a gendarme he retained only an iron constitution, a great sense of humor, and a vocabulary to make your hair stand on end.

It was Plantier who inadvertently, between apéritifs and jokes, revealed the course that I steered to overtake and capture the last of the treasure galleons. The most heavily laden of all. Every man has dreamed of heading that way. But I took a step in that direction. Then another, and another . . .

My Spanish galleon was the Société Générale bank at the avenue Jean-Médecin in Nice. That was where I went one Thursday morning to rent a safe-deposit box. I already had a business account with the Société Générale, but there was no vault at my branch. So it wasn't hard to rent one.

In the weeks that followed, I made three trips to my new safe-deposit box. One of those trips wasn't recorded in the visitors' logbook. I cased the vault inside and out.

Banks are very special places. They're as calm and quiet as

a church. These high priests carry out their financial rites in an atmosphere of contemplation and devotion. Their pale cheeks are closely shaven; their eyes are lifeless from years of exposure to the radiation from ingots and gems. Their hands are whiter than the hands of laundresses from the constant immersion in wads of holy images. Venerable defenders of holy capital, as ill paid as an Arab houseboy, they celebrate their divine services in three-piece suits, sober ties, and glistening shoes.

I can be a good listener when I'm eager to learn, and, brother, was I ever eager. I learned a lot that way. When I say, "Banks are very special places," it's no accident. Kafka lived through the heyday of bank tellers. Nowadays, when one of them makes a bookkeeping error — one that isn't in the bank's favor — the banks don't make it public. The banks have their own private gestapos. These are nothing like our Civilian Investigation Department, the cops that come from Paris, elegant, smelling of hair spray and after-shave lotion, with training in psychology. Those Parisian police walk right into the guy's apartment with an electric device for interrogation. They search his wife and poke around in the kids' diapers. Sometimes, they give the *mec* a few volts, and one-two-three: "You're lucky it wasn't you, wise guy. But just watch your step — we've got our eye on you."

I went on asking questions, often asking different people the same questions. Innocent questions, which I'd just leave hanging in the air. It was easy for me to bluff; I was the best listener you ever saw. Meanwhile, I took it all in, copying down information, drawing plans.

I paid special attention to alarm systems. The vault had been built in the early 1900s. I devoured all the brochures, copies of *Science et Vie,* banking magazines, technical literature. It was becoming more exciting all the time. I'd go from one bank to the next, breaking a fifty-franc note, then reversing the operation elsewhere.

I watched everything.

At five-thirty, when the employees took their apéritif, I was the most regular customer at the sidewalk cafés around the banks. And the information began to flow in — some of it highly interesting, some worthless. I classified it as it came in.

Then one night my plans, both of them, took shape. They were serious — with drawing, photos, maps, lists of equipment, estimates of costs. The first plan was simple, inexpensive, fast. It required no expertise, no big expenses. The second plan was pure fantasy, madness, Ali Baba's cave. It was the heist of the century. I'd dreamed up the first in order to finance the second. Because the big job would require elaborate equipment.

Plan number one called for knocking over a fat little branch office on a quiet street in an affluent neighborhood. A vault on the ground floor under a fashion designer's studio. A safe made of the same steel as French mailboxes. We could crack the safe-deposit boxes in two minutes flat, and still have time for a coffee break.

Two two-man teams for the actual work, including the lookouts on the street. In twelve hours we could leave the premises with a small fortune — without getting our hands dirty, without a fuss.

The fashion designer's studio would be empty from Friday night to Monday. No concierge, no other tenants upstairs. All we had to do was walk in with the equipment on Saturday morning, cover all doors and windows with blankets, hook up a powerful blower to one of the air shafts, and settle down to the delicate work with the torch.

The oxygen lance is the magic wand of burglars. It's just a tube of soft steel containing a thread of ferric oxide. At one end, you plug in high-pressure oxygen; you heat the other end with a common blowtorch, and, when the tube becomes a reddish white, you turn on the oxygen. Then you can melt concrete by going over a given perimeter several times.

There are lots of drawbacks involved in using this lance. Minor ones, owing to the bulky equipment. Furthermore, you've got to keep far away from it, protecting yourself from the flame with an asbestos suit, so you can't expect any accuracy. Then, too, there's the enormous quantity of gas used — about six or seven cylinders of oxygen for a hole eighteen inches in diameter and twelve inches deep. Finally, the real drawback: smoke.

How could I tell you this much about my plans without mentioning Charlotte? She must have been seventy-eight years old when I met her, although she didn't look a day over sixty. Those were the days when I went around knocking on doors, appealing for donations on behalf of a certain nationalist movement. I wasn't exactly gifted in that sort of fast talk. I could steal, but I didn't know how to beg.

I was a veteran of the Indo-China War. The daughter of a government official, Charlotte had also lived in Indo-China for twenty years or so. Like everyone else, she'd acquired a taste for strong tea and opium.

An artificial paradise — that isn't my bag. But, since she'd offered it to me, I saw no reason to refuse. I took a puff on the bamboo pipe with her that very evening in a room decorated with Oriental furnishings.

"Don't go around begging," she told me. "Money is something that you either earn or steal."

Over the years, we became accomplices. She had been alone for a long time, and I got into the habit of visiting her fairly often. She made me play games — planning jobs, thinking up perfect crimes — like detective-story writers. We used to laugh till our sides ached.

It was only natural to let her in on my wild scheme. And shortly afterward, Charlotte rented a safe-deposit box at the Société Générale branch on the avenue Jean-Médecin. I taught her to use a miniature camera, a Minox. She became my first co-worker, snapping pictures, taking measurements, and gathering information about bank layouts. Actually, it was data that I'd already gathered by myself. But she got such a kick out of it that I let her do it over. On the other hand, there was a ton of information that she alone could acquire.

You know these old ladies — they're so worried about their money that they ask millions of questions. "Just how safe is your bank? And remember, young man, you'd better not tell me a pack of lies. I'm old enough to be your grandmother. Upstairs they told me that the vault was safe — naturally. But they just want my business. I'd like to know what *you* have to say about it. You're the one who's actually down here. Yes, I see that it's armored and very thick . . . Couldn't you move so that I can get a better look? All right, you're down here in the daytime, and you look pretty husky — but who watches it at night? Are you down here at night, too? I know that you've got to sleep — I'm not finding fault with you. It's just that nobody's watching the vault at night. Does the vault fill up with water automatically in case of burglary — like the Banque de France? Why are you laughing? What's so funny? *My life savings are in that safe!* It may not be very much, but it's every sou that I have to my name. Where's the alarm? Come on, show me; I want to see everything. What do you mean? Upstairs? *Upstairs?* I don't care about alarms upstairs — *my money is down here!* . . . What's that you say? You've got to get past the alarm upstairs in order to get in here? Most of the walls are wired with alarms, you say? Here, have a cookie. I'm glad that most of them are wired. I wish all of them were. How come some are wired and some aren't? . . . You say there's only one that isn't wired? And why is that? . . . It's too thick, armored, impenetrable. I hope so, for your sake! I know that my questions are driving you crazy. Do you live around here? . . . In the Madeleine quarter? Well, if you've told me a lot of fibs, I'll make you the laughing-stock of the neighborhood. Did you see which safe-deposit box is mine? Well, don't let it out of your sight. That's what you get paid to do — not to stand there and say, 'What, again?' "

She put no valuables in her safe-deposit box — only choco-lates. Charlotte was rather frail-looking, with a face that was as withered and wrinkled as if she'd spent the whole winter in a pickle jar. But her pale blue eyes reflected great tenderness. If God is one of the boys, Charlotte must be up there with Him.

So, thanks to her, I accumulated a fantastic amount of addi-tional information. For my part, I was practically certain that there was no seismic or ultrasonic monitoring system, and I had a good reason for coming to that conclusion. I had concocted a big alarm clock with an ear-shattering ring and placed it in my safe-deposit box. Ten tries, all set for midnight. And ten times out of ten, nothing had happened to disturb the nocturnal calm of the bank or the neighborhood. The hitch was — the walls. According to Charlotte's information, one of them wasn't wired with an alarm. From what the vault clerk had told her, this wall was so heavily armored that to pierce it, you'd need to blow up the whole neighborhood. Which wall was it?

In any event, the job was feasible. The vault had a weak spot if I decided to break through the wall. Because that wasn't the only solution. Once I'd managed to go down to my safe-deposit box without the vault clerk entering my name in his logbook. The basement was vast, and the vault took up only one small part of it. I could certainly find a hiding place and wait there until the bank closed. With a man on the inside, things are much easier. At this stage in my planning, however, I was mainly concerned with entering the vault through the cellar of an adjoining building — either the house in which the bank concierge lived or the store that was wedged into the Société Générale building.

At that point my number one objective was to learn a bit about the wall devices. How did they operate? How were they hooked up? Were they set off by vibrations or by perforation?

When I think back to that time, even though it wasn't so long ago, I can't quite describe my frame of mind. I was obsessed. I had deserted my store. I was fed up with all that. I wanted to puke every time I thought about that row of stores: the shop where they sold fine wines, the dry-goods store, the shoe-maker's, and a small branch of the Société Générale. That little shopping center, just off the Route de Marseille — at that noisy intersection — facing a small parking lot. Across the way was a stop for the La Vallière bus, which runs from the Nice water-front out to the airport or to Saint-Laurent on the other side of the Var River. To the right of my store was a small clinic, where Audi worked.

It was a little shopping center like all the others. A place where everybody knew each other, where everybody smiled and said hello. Where everybody seemed so friendly . . . except there was anguish so intense that I couldn't sleep some nights.

The worst part came toward evening, when I went over the day's receipts. I'd dreamed of conquering the world, and there I was, behind a damned cash register, counting a handful of fuckin' change. Then there was that damned broad who knocked at the door. The store was closed and my mind was already far, far away. But that broad didn't give a damn. "Why do my pictures always come out so fuzzy?" she asked, right through the door. "I bought my camera from you!" Yes, there were hundreds of unrelated details, trivial incidents, that made me break out into a cold sweat, those hundreds of little fragments that wound up forming a whole picture. You can't explain that to yourself.

So I just shrugged and looked around. Low-ceilinged, the store was half-shop, half-office. I wondered how long I could hold out with all those invoices, those orders, those framed photos, those weddings, those interviews for the local newspapers . . .

I shrugged again and left the store in the hands of my manager. I headed up to The Wild Geese, near Bézaudun. I went for long walks in the woods with my Doberman pinschers, Parka and Vespa. I perfected my plan. I tailored it to my specifications. I worked the plan into the framework of my own life situation.

And then I asked myself: How the hell did you ever get yourself into this mess?

CHAPTER 3

Have You Always Been a Bandit?

I SPENT the last year of my childhood fifteen hundred meters high in the French Alps. The Germans had just deported my godfather, Uncle Aristide, for being too friendly with the British. And, on the other side of the Alps, other friends of the British were busy hanging his cousin for being too friendly with the Germans. It was all a big game for grownups.

I played games with Prince Eric beneath the glaciers, in the snow, in the middle of forests. We dammed up mountain streams, used the brittle slate of ravines for sliding ponds, and carved our initials in the bark of the fir trees.

Like all the others, my boarding school had gone over to the German schedule. After five o'clock mass, the whole morning was devoted to classes. Then, as soon as we'd had our daily meal of artichokes, out we went into the snow, wind, or cold, regardless of the temperature. In the morning we washed in the snow because the water pipes were frozen. But nobody ever caught a cold; nobody ever got sick. Sure, our hands were chapped and we cried with pain some nights when the feeling returned to frost-numbed hands and feet. Before bed, we had to say our evening prayers in memory of those fallen at Chad or Stalingrad. There was a Gregorian chant, a pastoral symphony, or a hymn to joy in the chapel every morning and night.

But then summer came, and I boarded the bus that took me to the town of Gap.

My mother was waiting for me. She looked me over right away for lice, scrubbed me in the kitchen sink with a coarse brush, then took me to the hospital to have my cuts treated. Good as new, I came walking back into the century of idiots.

It was a fine summer all the same.

On August 15, 1944, I was with my family in Sisteron to celebrate an aunt's birthday. At noon a neighbor came rushing in. "The Anglais have landed!" she shouted.

The word "Anglais" was used to cover a multitude of sins. The Americans were Anglais; de Gaulle was an Anglais; Rudolf Hess was an Anglais; even Rommel and Badoglio were Anglais. Well, at exactly 3:00 P.M., while everybody was digesting the big lunch — boom! The Anglais bombarded the town. They damned near leveled the place!

Why did they do it? There was no good reason. Just out of spite.

There were all of six German soldiers stationed at the fort, but they hardly ever stayed at their post. They spent the whole damned war in the same French homes. And the British were well aware of the situation.

So six days later, with five hundred fewer inhabitants, the town welcomed the new occupying army.

"*Vive les Anglais!* Good morning!" The crowd yelled in English.

"We're French, you idiots!" one soldier shouted back.

"*Vive la France!*" the people replied.

That year was also marked by my first great love. How beautiful Nicolajaque was, with her twelve golden years.

Coming back from mass one Sunday, I saw Jean M. grab her by the hair and start swinging her around like some kind of top.

"Little *collabo!*" he kept saying.

The blond girl didn't even cry.

Do you remember her, Jean? Do you remember how lovely she was? I had your head pinned to the ground and was going to kill you if you didn't say you were sorry. And that sweet little angel asked me to let you go.

Sure, you were my pal, Jean. But I needed Nicolajaque for the years to come; the color of her hair helped me to remember that year. It was the end of a world.

The Marist secondary school — my first jail. What makes a place into a prison, anyway? Am I really in jail now as I write these lines? Isn't prison simply the constraints imposed on you by family, society, neighbors?

Why does that school remain a shadowy place in my memory? Probably because it marked the break from a world to which I'd grown accustomed, a world of which I've never rid myself. Yet I should have been happy. There were all kinds of games — roller skating, Ping-Pong, miniature golf, and, wonder of wonders, actual plays staged with costumes and scenery. But there never was a great game for little men, like the mountain games we'd had the year before. We wanted games that involved danger, struggle, tears. The Marist school offered us nothing but phony games for rich kids. They didn't try to make us into sissies, but it was a far cry from the Alps.

We had to wear nice little uniforms like naval officers. I enjoyed that. It was a kind of battle dress. And then there was the smell of baking bread that hung about the immense corridors of the school. I've smelled that same odor in every prison where I've done time. I've grown used to it now.

One Sunday I'd been punished, so I ran away. It was my first breakout. For the sake of Nicolajaque's pretty eyes. Neither the head watchman at the front door nor the high wall studded with broken glass could discourage me.

I went running past the head watchman. He tried to catch me . . . Wham! He landed flat on his back. He'd somehow managed to break a leg.

My family "cops" brought me back, and, as the tuition was high, the school grudgingly allowed me to stay. But their hostility enabled me to taste forbidden pleasures, for they locked me in a big sun-filled room with one table and a bench. There I could daydream to my heart's content. And masturbate quite innocently. (It wasn't until some time later that a fat, red-faced man informed me that masturbation led to insanity.)

Oh, the joys of solitary confinement! At the far end of that room was a glazed door shrouded in mystery. In no time I managed to remove a pane of glass and slip through the opening. I found the school's whole collection of banned books there. That was my first "job."

I can still remember that fag Daguse saying, "I know, it's rough here. But we'll make a man out of you."

Meanwhile, providence must have put that forbidden library there for the benefit of incorrigible daydreamers, runaways, and simpletons.

There, in my first cell, I met the most exciting friends of my childhood. Elsa la cavalière; Gilles de Rais; Jeanne la papesse; Captain Conan, vagabond of the stars; and Tarzan. With Alain Gerbault, I sailed toward the sun; with Monfreid, I sold black slaves to the Arabs; with Giono, I enjoyed myself like a king; with Céline . . .

But I also recall the first slap I received. Uncle Justin gave it to me. I suppose I'd been slapped a few times before that, but I remember only this one.

I was in Gap for the summer. It was June 22, 1940. Jeannette came running in with the news. "The radio says it's the armistice . . ."

I can see her now, like a blond gazelle, taking the shortcut past the spring and the gooseberries, across the meadow below the farm. She was shouting and waving her arms. And Ponette, our dog, came bounding after her, thinking that Jeannette was playing.

Ponette was like me — she didn't quite understand the meaning of grownups' words. We'd heard the word "armistice" so often that we couldn't mistake it. We'd collected all those tin cans for the war effort. And the great tide of history, with dates and songs to back it up, made our destiny clear: armistice meant victory.

"It's the armistice!" I shouted gladly. "We've won the war!"

Wham! I got a smack in the face.

Right away my mother started trying to make me drink a glass of water. Every time she was very worried about me, she made me drink a glass of water and covered my shoulders with a blanket. But I didn't feel like a glass of water. I wanted a bottle of soda. Wham! I got another smack in the face.

God almighty, what a day!

When it came to kids and women, he packed a wallop, that Uncle Justin. He should have been at the front like the others — that was why he blew his stack.

I was fond of Uncle Justin. Like a chameleon, he could harvest wheat and pitch hay in the Alps, then go to fancy moving picture houses in Marseille or Hyères. He wore brightly colored shirts, and his trousers were pressed like razor blades. His shoes were as supple and light as socks. The flannel cummerbund worn by the village men wasn't for him. Even when plying his trade as a house painter, he dressed like a gentleman. What was more, he could sing like Tino Rossi. That was how he charmed my mother.

She had hired him to repaint her store. Before he finished,

she'd fallen for him. I got a father out of the deal. I also got my share of beatings.

Yes, I loved you, Uncle Justin. I loved you, but with the guilt and sadness of winning by a low blow. Because I'd managed to keep for myself the woman we'd shared for fifteen years — my mother, your wife. It isn't always fun to win, especially when the loser is somebody you love.

We should have kept on laughing, like the time you farted in bed and then pulled the covers over my head. Or when we made believe that we were trying to pick up the same girls just so that, afterward, we could wink and give each other a playful elbow in the ribs.

I'd lost my real father when I was three years old. I'd never gotten to know him. So I don't feel sorry about him the way I do about Uncle Justin. I don't remember my real father. Not even the beatings they claim he gave my mother and the fellows who asked her to go dancing on Saturday nights. I never knew my father, but I can imagine him from all the legends that I heard as a boy. Mostly stories about brawls. It's good to grow up with legends — I can endow my father with all kinds of virtue.

When I cross a bridge, they tell me that he's the one who built it. And that fine house and that road . . . He'd even done time in jail. With Uncle Aristide, one of his brothers, he'd beaten up two policemen. It seems that they had taken the braver of the two gendarmes and swung him against the ceiling. My father received a three-month sentence. Those were the good old days; now it would be three years minimum.

I kept his revolver, a Smith & Wesson .38, for a long time. I even used it on somebody when I was about eight or nine. We were waiting for the big kids outside the school yard. They had just received their elementary school diplomas. We pelted them with lumps of coal. Later, one of them, faster than the others, caught me in downtown Hyères. But suddenly I wheeled around, with my pistol aimed at his belly. He stopped in his tracks. Just like in the movies. He even put his hands up and backed away.

Police Sergeant Moretti happened to be going by. He took the gun away and dragged me home by the collar.

"Have you always been a bandit?" the sergeant asked.

"No! Ask my mother," I replied.

She thought I was a nice little boy. "He's so polite! You should see how sweet he looks in his black velvet suit!"

She forgot, but I didn't.

Have you forgotten about the *raille,* that constant war of kids in the south of France? The big ones against the little ones. The boys from Laragne against the ones from Montéglin. Those from Madrague against the boys from Grotte-Roland. One school against the other; one social class against the other.

Nowadays, when one of those gangs springs up, people call the police. They talk about juvenile delinquents, the influence of Hollywood movies.

Is the day coming when every man will become a policeman, where kids will dream about consumption or productivity?

I must have been separated from the Laragne district gang too soon. Because after the Marist school, I went to the public school in Hyères, where my mother had moved in order to conceal her romances as a widow. I kept up my little war with the kids from the school in the Paul-Long district, or with the boys in the old part of town, or with the creeps from the public school. Only, *I was keeping the war up all alone.* Oh, I had friends all right, and good ones at that. What's more, we're still friends thirty years later. But when the time comes to fight, you can't find anybody. It isn't a question of cowardice or apathy.

They have another way of thinking, one that's more intellec-
tual, more sophisticated. They play tennis, learn to cheat at
cards, yielding now and then to the temptation of a burglary.

At thirteen, I was a real yokel, five years behind everybody
else. So it took me a full four months to get myself tossed out
of the *lycée*. I didn't know the rules. In no time flat, I got myself
the seven different warnings required for expulsion. In most
cases, I didn't understand what was happening. As far as I
could see, only the last two warnings were justified. They remain in my memory like a symbol.

We had blacks from the Ivory Coast at our *lycée*. During the
recess, one of them started to bother a girl friend of mine,
Claudia, our gym teacher's daughter. Like a valiant knight, I
mounted my steed and charged at the black. We belted each
other for fifteen minutes. Finally, Claudia's father pulled us
apart and gave each of us a warning. A few weeks later, the
same kid called me a lousy wop because I couldn't vault over
the gym horse. I let him have it. Result: two warnings at once,
and I got myself expelled. The irony of the story is that while
I was off fighting in Indo-China (for some other stupid ideal of
mine), that same girl got herself knocked up by a black. Probably the same guy.

Albert Spaggiari, the embittered victim of an unhappy childhood? Ridiculous. I've been unhappy, really unhappy, but I've
also been happy.

There have been wonderful colors throughout my life. I've
known fire, sunshine, laughter, and song. There have been
manly handshakes, women's bodies, punches. I've gone down
roads under torrential rains and other, sunken roads in the dust
of summer. Prison? I've had some of the most beautiful daydreams in the filthiest jails.

When they gave me solitary confinement at the French

army's stockade in Hanoi, with my hands chained to the wall, my feet in irons, lying on the concrete, with four liters of water in the morning and a small, round loaf of bread to last four days, I sang.

There are some things worse than doing time. Why else would a guy go back to prison once he's cut his initials on the wall?

CHAPTER 4

Mercury's Smile

REAL LONELINESS must be what I see in the eyes of my dogs when I leave them. True loneliness is also when you don't even want to try to reassure anybody. You put down your shovel, your shotgun, and, on a Wednesday morning, you head down from Bézaudun to the city.

It was early morning. I was on the verge of depression. This wasn't the first time I'd hit rock bottom. And, as usual, I needed to snap myself out of it. I got downtown about eight o'clock. After reaching the Société Générale, I went around the block a few times, waiting for the bank to open. But I soon got fed up walking around, so I headed down the avenue Jean-Médecin and just kept on walking aimlessly.

A quarter of an hour went by, and I entered the Café de la Mairie.

Just on impulse. I almost never went to that bistro. I leaned my elbows on the zinc bar and ordered a cup of light coffee. I don't drink my coffee light as a rule. That was when Mercury, prince of thieves, smiled at me for the first time.

Standing at the bar next to me, an old bourgeois talked to the proprietor in a loud voice, gesturing. "So she says to me, 'That would really be something!' And I asked her, 'What? What would be something?' 'Can't you just picture yourself down in the Métro all alone with five Arabs going up to the place de la Californie? It's not that I'm a bigot or anything, but . . .' "

"What do you mean — Métro?" I asked. Actually, I didn't give a damn; I was just trying to relax a little.

This man, a baker or something, immediately turned to the other man standing at the bar of the café.

"Hey, this fellow must be new in town. They're planning to build a subway in Nice; haven't you heard?"

"A subway? I thought they couldn't build anything underground in Nice, on account of the Mediterranean."

"Jesus Christ! Where did we get this guy from? Haven't you ever seen the sewers? They aren't underground, I suppose?"

"You mean, here in Nice they have big sewers like Paris?"

"Of course they do, you big dunce. You can go from the avenue de Saint-Sylvestre clear up to the place de la Californie via the sewers."

"That's nothing," another man said, sneering. "You can drive a truck through the place de la Victoire sewer."

God almighty! Here I'd been racking my brains over thousands of plans. How could I have overlooked the sewers? That upside-down city, that gigantic anthill, that enormous Swiss cheese I'd walked over for years?

And that wall, damn it! The damned wall that was so thick, so strong, they hadn't even bothered to install alarms . . . That wall had to be the one with no adjoining building, the one that faced the sewers!

According to my survey, only one of the walls faced the sewers. Another might adjoin the cellar under the concierge's apartment, and the other two formed walls within the basement of the bank.

The winter was over. Warm sunlight smacked me in the face. What a beautiful day!

And it wasn't over. Mercury was going to smile on me a second time. Twice in the space of a few minutes.

I went back to the Société Générale and saw the most beautiful sight in the world. A guy in faded blue coveralls and a pair of hip boots stood in the middle of a circle of conical yellow markers. He was lifting the manhole cover on the rue Deloye and getting ready to go down into the sewer. My heart skipped a beat. According to my maps — I knew them by heart — the vault was located right in line with that manhole.

I stood, fascinated, in front of the sidewalk oyster bar outside the *brasserie.* I slowly fished a cigar out of my pocket, then a box of matches. I was taking my time. I wanted to watch everything. A second sewerage inspector had just emerged from a light delivery truck. He wore the same outfit as the other. *Zut!* It was easy as pie. What an idiot I'd been for thinking it had to be a highly complicated job! Christ, I'd almost given up because it looked so complicated.

I finally got my cigar lit. I crossed the rue de l'Hôtel-des-Postes. Then the rue Deloye. The manhole was located right in the middle of the street, at a pedestrian crosswalk. The sewer ran parallel to the street and wasn't very wide. I paced off the distance to the wall of the bank and calculated that we'd have to dig a tunnel about three and a half yards long. (This turned out to be all wrong.)

A few seconds later I was crossing the marble floor of the Société Générale, heading for the vault attendant. He logged my name, my number, the time, and date. Then he pressed a button, and I was allowed to go downstairs to the vaults. My enthusiasm went soaring upward when I saw the perfect alignment of the gleaming armor plate. Echoing in my brain were the voices of bank tellers boasting, as they drank their evening apéritifs, "With the deposits from Galeries Lafayette, we've got more than forty million francs in the vault some weekends!"

Forty million francs! Oh, Jesus!

I opened my briefcase. I'd brought a second alarm clock. This one was a regular fire alarm. I set it to go off at midnight by remote control with the other clock, then shut my safe-deposit box. When those two babies went off, the whole block might shake.

I was sure they didn't have a seismic or ultrasonic alarm. People had told me so over and over. But I couldn't really believe it unless I did some more checking.

Then I knew I had something. There was no reason why the job shouldn't work. All I had to do was organize things. Get down to business. Step number one: come up with an oxygen lance.

Setting up two heists at the same time wasn't easy, believe me. If it were all that simple, everybody and his brother would be doing it. But I didn't know just *how* hard it was going to be. I mean, my mistake lay in thinking that the hardest part was done, that it would be smooth sailing the rest of the way. I was wrong again.

You see, I'm not a professional bank robber. I'm an adventurer. That's not the same thing. It amounts to the difference between an airline pilot and a stewardess.

I needed an oxygen lance, no more, no less. That was all I could think about.

I told myself that the problem could be solved. After all, didn't Europe have a Common Market? All I needed was the classified section of the phone book. They had them in any good hotel. And what about the post office? Would they have a phone book? Yes, there was one at the post office! Great! I had a notebook. I copied down everything between Paris and Marseille: hardware stores, wholesalers, construction companies, demolishers, engineering consultants, compressed-air dealers.

After that, I had letterhead stationery printed up.

"Hello, this is the C.M.B.P.T. Corporation. Do you sell oxygen lances? We've got a big rock in our basement and we've got to break it up. We thought of using dynamite but the neighbors didn't like the idea."

"Oxygen lance? What's that?"

Bye.

Two weeks later, after eight thousand phone calls.

"Hi! This is the C.M.B.P.T. Corporation calling . . ."

"You hit me at the wrong time. I had one in stock last week. I'm all out of them now. Go see Dushnok on the rue de la Tordue."

But Dushnok had gone into bankruptcy.

I couldn't sleep; I couldn't talk; I couldn't eat. One morning as I walked wearily around a building that was being demolished (I was trying to learn the tricks of the trade) I bumped into a crazy grocer. The guy sounded like a walking encyclopedia. He gave me the address of a guy who tinkered with cutting equipment and made oxygen lances of his own for salvaging wrecked ships.

But he'd moved without leaving a forwarding address.

I wasn't going to drop my plans for lack of a damned cutting tool! I'd find the damned thing if it took me a hundred years.

CHAPTER 5

The Ectoplasm

NOTHING MUCH HAPPENED until one evening, when I was having a drink with some friends, an Ectoplasm in a violet blue suit whispered in my ear, "Want to take a little trip to Africa in the next few days? I know somebody who might have some dollars for you. Lots of dollars . . ."

I couldn't have cared less about his dollars.

"All I want is an oxygen lance," I replied, stifling a yawn. "Know anybody who's got one?"

"I've got one."

I was so astonished that I couldn't speak. Who the hell was this character, anyway?

"Are you serious or what?" I asked after a full minute's silence.

"I'm serious."

Calm down, I told myself. Musn't let this guy know that I'd give anything for that equipment.

"*Garçon!* Another round!" I shouted, fishing a cigar out of my pocket. I spent a long time lighting it. Then I blew smoke upward and turned to the Ectoplasm.

"Go ahead, talk. I might have a deal for you." I rubbed my thumb and forefinger together. "How much?"

"A thousand francs, maybe more. I'll have to ask . . ."

We exchanged phone numbers.

"Waiter! Cancel that order!"

That night I got all my stuff out again: maps, photos, estimates . . . and I began dreaming.

The next day, I pulled the plans back out and added some finishing touches. And I waited. I waited for a damned phone call that wouldn't come. By the third day, I didn't leave the phone at all. I took it with me even when I went into the toilet. On the fifth day, I started calling friends out of town just to ask them to call me back. I had to be sure that my phone worked. Nothing was wrong. That son of a bitch just wouldn't call me.

By the end of the week, I'd given up. One more dead end. Two days later, the son of a bitch called. When I recognized his voice, I felt like slamming the receiver down in his face. Instead, I agreed to meet him in a bar.

"Sorry, but it's impossible to get that tool. I missed one by just a few hours. I actually went all the way to Paris, trying to get it for you."

I started toying with my drink. I figured it wouldn't be long before he tried to hit me up for money. Seeing that I remained silent, he went on, "Look, I've got something better."

"Better? How?"

"I mean a team of experts, if you're planning a real job. And as for equipment, they've got something better than an oxygen lance. It's the best son-of-a-bitching tool there is."

"You mean a laser? You wouldn't be trying to put one over on me, would you?"

The Ectoplasm's face went white as a sheet. He looked like a dish towel after it has been washed in a miracle detergent. His hamlike hands moved a lot as he swore on a stack of Bibles that he'd made inquiries about me, that he knew perfectly well who he was dealing with. That he was getting pretty involved just putting me in touch with that team . . . the best team in the business. He kept harping on that.

I'd heard that line before. You spot a guy who's looking for fancy equipment. Preferably some yokel. You take him for a bundle.

He knew that I wasn't going to jump at just anything. He made another try. "Talk it over with them. Maybe you can make a deal. You can always back out if they don't talk turkey."

I studied the bottom of my glass for a moment. In a way, the guy wasn't all wrong: What did I have to lose? I was a little hot under the collar because things weren't going the way I'd planned. I finally said I'd take him up on his suggestion. He got to his feet and told me that he was going to arrange a meeting; he'd let me know the time and place.

"When?" I asked. "In a day, a week, two weeks?"

"Fairly soon."

Answers like that always make me see red.

"If I don't get a call from you in the next ten days, I'm going to put your face through the wall!"

And the waiting started. And with it, weariness, worry. And then I got my brainstorm. The idea was really quite simple: it called for dropping plan number one. Just plain forget it. Actually, it had been designed solely to finance the second plan. If that team of his was all that it was cracked up to be they'd certainly be able to tackle plan number two: the big, fat Société Générale bank on the avenue Jean-Médecin.

I burned everything connected with the first plan. And, for the hundredth time, I pulled out the second one. I reworked it from scratch. This time my planning was methodical. I had to have something really solid to show if I expected to dictate my terms.

Meanwhile, Charlotte had managed to plant a special radio

in Ali Baba's cave. It was a radio set on the same frequency as my walkie-talkies. (She Scotch-taped it under the table inside the vault.) And, for most of Tuesday night, I played Radio Monte-Carlo over my transmitter.

I was still obsessed with the idea of a seismic or ultrasonic alarm. These experiments had to add some weight to my theory.

On Wednesday morning, Charlotte and I went down to the vault together. She didn't want me to go with her. We argued about it, but that didn't get us anywhere. I wanted to be there in order to cover her when she removed the radio from underneath the table. Charlotte was old; she just didn't understand the risk. The whole thing was just a game for her. If she was caught removing the radio, it wouldn't take them long to make the right connections. And that would be the end of my heist. But everything went smoothly.

I decided to stay downtown that day. My plans were set. I ate in a little restaurant on the place de l'Armée-du-Rhin. Afterward, I strolled through the Old Town, around the flower market.

"Hello, there, Monsieur Spaggiari. Good to see you. It's been a long time since I've seen you."

It was a former customer. I'd done his two daughters' weddings. I mean, I'd taken the wedding pictures.

"Aren't you the one who's looking for an oxygen lance to clear the rock out of your cellar? Do you see the building under construction over there? Come along with me. There are two bundles of the stuff. It's been lying around for three weeks or more. Nobody knows who it belongs to. You can just take the stuff."

"Really?"

"Of course."

I swear to God that's exactly how it went, almost word for word. Here I'd been hunting for an oxygen lance all over France, and suddenly two of them fall into my lap. And free of charge, yet!

Two days later, I got a call from Ectoplasm. We arranged a meeting. He showed up late, claiming that he'd been stuck in traffic.

He told me to get into his beat-up old jalopy, and we went roaring off toward the seashore. To a restaurant. Whether I was headed for a bargain or a pack of headaches, I still couldn't tell.

CHAPTER 6

The Gang from Marseille

ECTOPLASM waddled in like a trained seal. I made him go ahead of me. Everyone at the table turned around to look at his pasty face. Then they watched me enter from behind the coat racks. I wanted them to know that I was in no hurry, that I was just sightseeing. I had lots of time. I could take it or leave it.

The restaurant faced the beach. It was fairly big. Thirty tables or so, all vacant except for one. They must have rented the whole damned place. At least, that was the hunch I had at the time. Afterward, I learned that the restaurant just stayed closed on Thursdays. I learned that friends of friends had agreed to arrange the meeting.

There were four of them. That rubbed me the wrong way. I'd been expecting one guy all by himself. The boss. Not a whole damned tribe.

We exchanged a few words. The usual crap. They all had that same smile. Like salesmen who never missed a sale. I felt about as much at ease as a chicken in a poultry market. After a few minutes, they had me. I fell under the spell. Those guys were from Marseille, a city that very few people know. But I knew it.

Marseille is a city totally unlike its image in books. The door of the Orient, the tall stories, Marius and Caesar, the pimps

with long sideburns and fleshy jowls, the red-light district
. . . that's all phony. The Marseillais are a different race, one
that has come from everywhere to reap the friendship, the deep
joy made of little nothings, and the beauty of simple things. A
city you've got to grow up in to really know. A place with smells
unlike any in the world. In my lifetime of travel, colonial wars,
adventures, and prisons, I've always bumped into a Marsellais,
warm as sunlight, friendly and sincere.

"You're all from Marseille, right?"

"No, le Vieux is from Castapiagne."

Pierre was the first to shake my hand. Pierre was the leader.
The others introduced themselves. Their names, borrowed from
the Gospel, were aliases. That was the rule, and a good one.
Nobody ever broke it. Nobody except me. I stayed Bert Spaggiari. Naturally, they were quick to nickname me Bertie. I
wasn't altogether pleased to get this diminutive back again, and
I told them so.

First, we downed a string of anisettes. Want a cigarette?
Some olives? Another drink? They fussed over me as if I were
a young widow with a fortune to invest. I enjoyed myself. Even
if they went a little overboard, I couldn't help liking the guys.
The only one at the table who didn't fit in was Ectoplasm. He
was different — he annoyed me. Even before I knew him, he
annoyed me. Some people are like that.

Then we ate. I don't remember the menu, but I clearly recall
Pierre, the leader. After looking me over for a long time, he said
that he never accepted a partner unless he'd seen him eat first.
Eating, he said, was a life function that forced the individual to
drop all pretense. The way I ate must have pleased him, because
it set up a good relationship right away.

Next, they started trying to outdo each other with those
exaggerations typical of the Marseillais.

"Look at le Vieux; he hardly eats anymore. He must be dying."

Le Vieux was the one from Castapiagne, supposedly named Joseph. About six feet tall, he was bald as a cue ball, pot-bellied, and straight as a ramrod. As he sprang to his feet, his paunch hit the edge of the table. Hurriedly, everyone began righting the fallen bottles.

"Go fuck yourselves!" le Vieux snarled.

The scene was typical for crooks from Marseille. Even in the most dangerous circumstances, they had to clown.

Seated to Pierre's right was Jean, alias Bouche d'or. His face long and his eyes like a Saint Bernard's, he reminded me of my priest when I'd been a kid. But his looks were deceiving. He was actually the gang's treasurer, the one who would finance the job.

Waiters came to clear the table. Then they brought us coffee. A silence fell over the room. Although we'd talked only about the weather up to then, we'd never stopped watching one another. Now, each of us was looking absently at the tablecloth, sweeping the bread crumbs into little piles.

Through the bay windows, the sea looked gray, leaden, as if the sun had fallen on its face while climbing the hill of Saint-André. I fished a cigar out of my pocket and took my time trimming it. Mathieu coughed. Mathieu was the fourth person in the group. I knew that they expected me to do the talking. You can cough as much as you want, Mathieu. I'd learned to think fast the day I was born. It's become automatic. My whole life's been one big tightrope act. Yes, you can cough away, Mathieu.

Finally, I lit my cigar.

"You can quit trying to kid me with that laser story," I said, blowing a smoke ring their way. "Somebody pulled that one on me when I was five years old."

Pierre was the only one who met my eyes. The others looked at Ectoplasm, who went on staring into his coffee cup.

"You're right — we don't have any laser. But you can count us in on the job, if that's what you're wondering about," Pierre whispered, leaving a space between each word.

Pierre was a bright boy. You could spot that a mile away. He had an intelligent, straightforward look. You could tell that he had his feet on the ground. I liked him right away.

"Now the question is — can we work together? It's your caper, so you do the talking."

"Fine," I said.

At this point, the whole gang began breathing again. Before a job everyone has lots of wild ideas. These guys were no exception. And I'd just offered them some kind of guarantee.

Pierre jerked his chin in Ectoplasm's direction.

"He told us that you're planning a very big heist."

"He wasn't lying. A vault with four thousand safe-deposit boxes. No guards. No alarms. Thirty to forty million francs. You get in through the sewers."

Thirty to forty million francs.

They looked at one another, each man trying to see if he alone had heard that figure.

Le Vieux looked up at the ceiling, protecting his head with his arms as if he expected it to collapse on him.

Bouche d'or leaned toward me.

"How much did you say?"

"Thirty or forty."

"Million?"

"Million!"

"Where did you get your information?"

"Right from the horse's mouth. And there's bound to be more, if you're interested in stocks and bonds."

"Say the whole thing again."

I said it again.

Le Vieux moved his chair next to mine.

"Are you sure? I mean, really sure?"

Obviously, none of them had ever dreamed of anything that big. They were trying to imagine what that much money looked like. It took a while. They'd never had to count so high.

After the third brandy, the meeting degenerated into a laughing spree. The heist was just too big; nobody could get over it.

"Well, what do you say now, you big moron?" le Vieux said with a laugh, shaking Mathieu like the branch of an apple tree. "You didn't even want to come. Now what do you say?"

"What about the risks?"

"Going through the sewers? Don't be stupid. I've taken bigger risks doing my laundry."

"Yeah? We'll see."

"What do you mean, 'We'll see?'"

But le Vieux's enthusiasm slid off him like water off a duck's back. Dark, thickset, Mathieu had the eyes of a man who'd been through a lot but who could be depended on when the time came.

Pierre wasn't the only one who raised the question of alarms. I told him that I knew what I was talking about, that I'd been planning the job for months. He didn't press the point. This was only our first meeting. We'd schedule another talk, at which time we could go into the details.

I paid for another round of drinks, and the boys went on laughing about what they'd do with their millions. Even Mathieu this time. Like I told you, these guys were warm and friendly. Well, in that business everybody is warm and friendly.

Then the bistro door swung shut behind me and there I was, out in the sea breeze, alone with my own questions. My own doubts. Would the job work or wouldn't it? I thought it over from every angle. Now that I'd let the cat out of the bag, I hoped these guys were going to follow through. I hoped they were going to be brilliant. They had to pull it off somehow. There was no other choice. Well, I thought about a few other things as I was walking along the beach. I thought about the years that had gone by, about all the boats I'd missed. It isn't so hard to understand: I was a little drunk. It's not a good idea to be alone when you're only half-drunk.

I'm not always a robber. Being a thief isn't a permanent condition with me. It isn't something unchangeable, like the color of your eyes or your pubic hair. I'm only a robber when I'm in peak form or in the depths of despair. Stealing is a noble profession. When I'm sick, I act like some kind of a dog. I wait for somebody to throw me a bone. I sit up and beg. I lick my master's hand; I wait for his command; I think up things that he might need. Well, I'd been sick for a long time. For years, ever since I'd been unfairly sentenced after Dien Bien Phu, when a guy tore off my insignia and decorations, and some character covered with gold braid wouldn't let me go and die with my buddies. I'd been sick when they dragged Ali Mérina out to face the firing squad at Fort Saint-Nicolas. I'd been sick before . . .

Yet I'd gotten a good start in life. In fact, when I was ten, my godfather had hung a placard on my back: I AM A THIEF AND A LIAR, then brought me to school like that.

And what do you think happened? I suppose you think they threw stones at me. Well, you don't understand children if you think so. Because this is what they said: "We're amazed, Bertie. We thought you were too dumb for that."

It's tough, trying to rob your parents. You've got to learn to pick a lock, make wax impressions and copies of keys, climb walls, sneak in the room where your mother or father is sleeping.

And never be caught. Well, not until afterward. Except the

day that I deliberately let myself be caught so that my mother would want to give me her consent for the paratroops. And a few times I got nabbed through my own extravagance. Like when I bought too many emblems of French provinces for my collection.

Wham! My backside was smoking after the beating I'd got. And they'd sent me away to a farm in the Alps, where I worked in the fields all summer.

That summer vacation turned out to be one of the happiest of my youth. I can still smell the wheat and the hay, the chaff that I washed down with gulps of wine. I ate, drank, and worked like a man. Every evening we'd have a celebration. We'd really feed. We got plastered and sang at the top of our lungs. And every evening, without fail, I'd have a fist fight with the owner's son. It became such a ritual that as soon as the fight erupted, everyone stopped guzzling or dancing and formed a ring around us. They'd even place bets on us.

Oh, the smell of the wheat! Why the hell do we let life drag us back to the porcelain toilet bowls and asphalt pavement of the cities?

I guess I never understood. And what little I did understand I couldn't swallow. I live outside society. That's why this book shocks you.

CHAPTER 7

The Second Meeting with the Marseillais

TWO DAYS LATER I got together again with my prospective partners. This time there were seven of them. Naturally, I had to repeat the estimated total of the loot for the newcomers.

Right away Saint-Jacques, alias la Fouine, a guy as skinny as a rail with gray hair that hung down over his forehead, came to lend me a helping hand. He was trying to convince the others. "The haul would be big enough if we got even three or four million francs."

The rest of them looked at me out of the corner of their eyes, watching for my reaction.

"Not on your life!" I snapped. "If we hit for less than twenty million, I'd be disappointed." And I meant it.

Thomas, alias le Tombeur, a strong, handsome guy with a big smile, nudged another man with his elbow.

"Le Vieux, do you hear what I hear?"

"I sure do. And it's music to my ears."

Then Pierre came into the middle of the room. He raised his hands and called for silence. The court was in session.

"Go ahead, Bert. We're listening."

"We're going after a bank. The building has . . ." (I was about to say that it had frontages on three streets. I realized that there was no need to supply them with that bit of information for the time being.) "At night there's no watchman. The vault hasn't any seismic alarm or TV monitoring device. Three walls are bugged, but the fourth is so thick and strong that the insurance company hasn't insisted on installing an alarm. Now, this wall runs parallel to the city sewers, four or five yards away. That's where we're going to dig. I haven't actually inspected the sewers. I'll see about that once we've worked out the terms of our partnership."

Pierre began pacing back and forth. The others watched him. The silence was complete. Then he stopped.

"First of all, you tell me how you see the caper," said Pierre, pulling out a pack of cigarettes.

"All right, here it is. I supply the plan and a team with experience in tunneling and excavation. Also plumbers, welders, electricians. These people are pros. There will be seven of us in all. You, on the other hand, will be expected to provide the money, equipment, plus certain specialists. There would be a fifty-fifty split. Your team gets one half; my team gets the other."

"You mean, we don't split according to the number of men?"

"Right. We split by team — it's the easy way. You hand out your team's share any way you want."

He began pacing up and down again, only now he was scratching his ear as well.

"We'll see about that later on," he said casually.

"No, we settle it right now," I replied. "There are going to be plenty of technical problems. I want to be able to face them with a clear head."

I had the upper hand. My bargaining position was plenty strong, and I knew it. So did everyone else.

Pierre stopped his pacing and looked me straight in the eye.

From up close. Real close. His eyes had that fierce gleam where anger borders on amusement, intelligence on insanity.

I'd seen that look before in prison, twenty years earlier. I'd seen that look in René's eyes. At the time, France had sold out its commando units to the infidel and had thrown the last few survivors of those outfits into dungeons. The lesson had been highly instructive. And then René got himself knifed in the back one night.

Pierre clapped his hands as if to say: I'm taking the plunge. "All right, it's a deal. But there's one proviso. I have to like your boys or they're dropped. Agreed?"

As he said this, he stuck out his hand. I shook it. Hard. We'd just sealed the first part of a deal.

Afterward, we tried to work out a few technical questions. I wanted to know more about their potential. But the issue of burglar alarms kept cropping up. Alarms, alarms, alarms . . .

Finally, I got pissed off. "Damn it, I told you I spent nights ringing alarm clocks in that vault. I even had a damned transistor radio going full blast down there. Furthermore, nothing's stopping you from renting a safe-deposit box of your own and doing the same experiments."

My argument held water. What more did they need to know?

Finally they changed the subject. "Talk about the safe-deposit boxes."

"Prewar design, about fifty years old. The safe doors are about six feet by six feet and fifteen inches thick. Inside each strongbox are thirty to fifty individual safe-deposit boxes. Don't underestimate them — they're going to give us our biggest headache."

"No, our problem is going to be the alarm."

And, bang! The fireworks started again. Those bastards just

couldn't understand. They had a regular obsession with that goddamned alarm. What were these characters — some kind of morons? I came within an ace of blowing my top. Instead, I got up and walked away from the table. I took a cigar from my pocket. I lit it as calmly as possible. For a moment, all my energy was directed at one goal: lighting my cigar as calmly as possible. What the hell, I had to admit I'd been obsessed with the alarms myself. For weeks I'd thought of nothing else. All right, all right . . .

"Look, I'm telling you once more, I'm absolutely positive that there's no alarm. At any rate — and you know this better than I do — ninety-nine times out of a hundred when an alarm goes off, the police come; they check the premises fast; and they go away. Worse comes to worst, the cops hang around. They don't try to go into the vault until the two 'keys' are there. For that matter, most banks use time locks nowadays, so the police have to wait for the automatic opening. Now if you want to be absolutely sure, there's nothing to stop you from bugging the place with microtransmitters that cost twenty-five francs apiece in any radio appliance store. Just plant the sons of bitches around the bank and in the vault the day before the heist. I'll show you exactly what I'm talking about."

I went outside to get one of those bugs from my Land Rover. I explained how the gadgets worked.

"We're not leaving anything to chance. Even the police wavelengths. I know the central police frequency and the mobile stations. With two extra radios and the right frequency modulation we'll be all set."

I'd convinced them. I had the spiel down to a science. Right away, the atmosphere brightened. They started poking each other in the ribs. Thomas, le Tombeur, sparred playfully with the one named Hervé. Hervé was a slim blond fellow without a police record. Apparently, he'd had a fine education. To avoid the draft after completing secondary school, he'd volunteered to work in a former French colony in Africa. There, he saved the neck of a grateful crook and, without fanfare, drifted into the world of adventure.

It felt good in the café, so we lingered over the huge dinner until almost five o'clock.

Although we did reach an agreement on the terms of the split, Pierre still hadn't given the heist his final approval. Now he had to study my proposition and discuss it with Bouche d'or. He also had to draw up a tentative list of equipment. He couldn't give me a definite answer until he was sure of his funding and the availability of experienced people.

It was agreed that he wouldn't contact me until everything had been set up.

CHAPTER 8

Calling Out the Old Guard

THE MORNING AFTER that meeting, I woke up convinced that somehow the machinery was in motion and that nothing would ever stop it now. Even Pierre couldn't put on the brakes. The job was just too colossal, too gorgeous.

I shoved the dogs into the Land Rover and drove downtown. First I stopped for a coffee, then bought some cigars; afterward, I went to the post office on the place Grimaldi.

From the telegraph window there I sent a wire to Sixty-eight. In essence I was saying, "Call me back." We had our code, and he'd understand that it wasn't about some trifling job. I also cabled instructions for reaching me. There was no point in my wife's seeing him. That would only make her suspicious. She'd start asking me all kinds of questions.

I didn't want her involved in the job. For one thing, she wouldn't have gone along with it . . . there were promises I'd made. Anyway, it's a long story. Nobody likes long stories.

Next, I sat myself down in a café in the Old Town and wrote to Rico and Carlos. I didn't know where they were, so I sent the letter to a contact. There was a chance that the letter might take some time to reach them. On the envelope I wrote: *"Urgent, Fissa, Schnell, Presto, Hurry Up."*

Rico and Carlos: that's another long story. To put them in perspective, you should know that after the OAS and prison, Le Rouxel had sold his liquor store and, becoming a reporter, emigrated to Lisbon, where he offered his services to Ploncar d'Assac.

Portugal, even more so than Spain, was the European haven for all kinds of nationalists. Before the revolution, Portugal had tolerated the presence of all the former French collaborators and SS who either couldn't afford a ticket to South America or couldn't adapt to civilian life. But the revolution of the red roses cut a big swath in the ranks of those forget-me-nots.

Le Rouxel, an old right-wing campaigner, had felt the revolution coming for years. Before he died, he distributed his address books and notes to a few "mad dogs" of nationalism.

The son of a Portuguese colonist in Angola, Rico had been taken in by friends in Spain. He witnessed the exodus of the finest from their countries and the plight of those refugees over the past thirty years. Russians, Cossacks, Ukrainians, Croats, Indians, *pieds-noirs;** now they were being hunted all over Europe. Spain, their last hope, was herself succumbing to the fate of all the other European countries.

Then Rico and Carlos had gone all over Europe with Le Rouxel's address book. After a thousand refusals, a thousand closed minds, Rico tried me. Carlos, a Falangist who'd broken parole, came along with him.

"There's nothing else we can do but use our last reserves," they said.

I remember them that night, how the flickering light from the hearth played over their tortured faces. Both men waltzed with the ghosts of their dying world. Use our last reserves — *where?* For what cause, for what country, for what lofty ideal?

---

*Translator's note: Algerian-born Frenchmen.

They stayed at The Wild Geese for three days. After splitting enough firewood to last me a whole winter, they planted an olive tree, then left a note and vanished.

Sixty-eight, Rico, Carlos . . . I also needed Biki!

Biki's face has always stayed in my memory.

There I was, seated at a table at the back of some crummy little café. I looked around me in the morning silence. The pen, the writing paper, the anisette, a few boozers standing at the zinc counter. I recall mumbling to myself, "How idiotic life can be."

The confusion and chaos in my brain! A pal's face, a dusty old knapsack that seems to smile at you.

Biki was one of the close friends I depended on. I didn't have many close friends, so I looked after him. I remember exactly how we met. I was in Algeria and couldn't wait to get off the main *pistes* of Hoggar, which were choked with tourists. You know — those prisoners of the two-week paid vacation, bored stiff but snapping millions of pictures so that everybody back in Paris will think they're world travelers.

Not so long ago, a few courageous boys fought and died for that Sahara. Now, over those same sacred battlefields, endless lines of cars carry fat, western carcasses, with all their democratic boredom and selfishness.

The day before I met Biki I was in Tamanrasset. Which reminds me of an anecdote. It must have been five o'clock in the evening. I was walking around a hotel pool to get to the bar. Two white whores, lying on their bellies, the bras of their two-piece suits undone, were surrounded by young Arabs and were shooting their mouths off. Almost deliberately, one of these bitches made a remark as I went past her beach towel. Apparently in reply to a question, she'd said, "Well, of course!

The only good Frenchmen were the young people who supported the FLN* during the war."

I stopped in my tracks. I wasn't going to let that one go by
without a fight.

"Your young people were a bunch of cunts, just like you."

The girl scrambled to her feet angrily while trying to fasten
her bra. But before she hooked it, I gave her a hard slap in the
face. And then I went on my way again. One of the Arab boys
grabbed hold of my trouser leg. Another got up and came
rushing at me to defend his damsel's honor. I knocked the son
of a bitch on his behind twice before the others joined in.

At any rate, we all wound up at the police station. For once
I hit it lucky: the chief was an ex-paratrooper from the third
battalion, practically a brother.

In his report he wrote that the young lady in question had
been slapped for lewdly exposing her genitalia in public. And
the police chief and I spent the evening at the hotel, getting
ourselves soused and singing songs from the good old days. The
young Arab I'd punched came in, too, and drank with us because that white bitch, rotten to the core, wouldn't even let him
back in her room.

I left Tamanrasset the following afternoon with an awful
hangover. In fact, when I got behind the wheel of my Land
Rover, I couldn't find the gear shift. I'd climbed into the wrong
Land Rover. Finally, I got out onto the *piste* and drove. I drove
for hours. I love the desert like sailors love the sea. It's a kind
of a kingdom to me, my paradise. The Sahara is another planet.
You're out there with the nothingness, with yourself.

Around 8:00 P.M. I reached an incredible jumble of rocks and

*Translator's note: National Liberation Front (FLN), the Algerian Moslem move-
ment for independence from France.

gullies. The sun went down, cooling off the desert. But I knew that it would be worse the next day. The oven of the world really starts when you cross the Nigerian border. I decided to get out of that rock-strewn area of the desert.

Half an hour later, long before sunrise, I caught sight of a lone figure. No doubt a Targui. Even out there where a snake can't survive, the Tuaregs stroll around like they're on some kind of Paris boulevard. Lordly, supremely indifferent, they walk with an easy, athletic tread. It could only be a Targui; he hadn't even turned around to look at the car. An Arab or a black would have been up on the road asking for water.

I pulled the Land Rover over when I came abreast of him.

"*Salamalecoum,*" I said, greeting him in his own language.

"Fuck you!"

"Well, well."

He didn't stop. I shifted into drive to catch up with him.

"I thought you were a Targui. From close up, you look like a wop. What did you do — bust out of jail or something? Hey, look at me, for Christ's sake. What do I look like — some kind of tourist?"

He looked. When he smiled, it was as though he held a knife in his teeth. But there was something about him I liked.

"I busted out of jail in Italy. My name is Biki."

"Hop in."

Yes, his name was Biki. He was an Italian but spoke French without an accent. Short and slender, he had the delicate bone structure of a bird. There was something almost distinguished-looking about him.

For several minutes we drove through that rocky landscape in silence. Night comes quickly out there, like the tide in some narrow bays.

Our speedometer kept wavering between five and twenty-five

mph. Brakes, gas, speed, brakes, skid, spin in a circle, gas, brakes . . .

"Get off the road. You've got firmer sand to your right."

"Sounds like you know this area."

"I've been around here for three years."

"You work here?"

He simply shrugged.

"Then how do you live?"

"With the nomads or by sponging off tourists. Sometimes they hire me for a guide." Then, removing a cigar from the box next to him, he asked, "How are these cigars — any good?"

"Try one. See for yourself."

He snatched the box of matches from my hand and lit the stogy, drawing on it the way hashish smokers do.

"So you work as a guide for tourists, huh?"

"Yes. And when they're too damned moronic, I steal their money and tell them to get lost. Yesterday I was with some Dutchmen who bragged about stealing a jack from a stranded motorist."

He pulled out a wad of dollars and two passports.

"Want some?"

I shook my head. I didn't need his money. He stuffed the wad and passports back into his pocket.

"Those Dutch assholes won't need any either. I sent them to Ouljin. Ever been to Ouljin?"

No, I'd never been there.

"It's an isolated village somewhere between Hoggar and Tannezrouft. If they ever make it, they'll be lucky. In any event, they won't steal any more jacks in the Sahara. Stay to your left — that's *fechfech* over there. Get up on the highway. There's no more rock now, and the sand is rotten up ahead."

He puffed on his cigar and gave orders. He looked like a ship captain. Every now and then he squinted into the distance as though expecting reinforcements. I liked the guy.

At one point, I went off the highway, and the Land Rover bogged down in the sand.

"Too bad. We'll have to camp here for the night," I announced after trying vainly to get traction.

I opened the door and hopped down into the sand.

"Come on. Let's set up the butane stove and cook some grub."

Biki looked at me in amazement. Then he started cracking his knuckles as though he were about to play a Liszt prelude on the dashboard.

"This is the first time anybody's ever pulled the breakdown routine on me. We're miles from the nearest house," he said, getting out of the car, the stump of the cigar stuck between his lips.

"What's on the menu today?" he asked.

"Nobody you know. Here, open these two cans. After that, start setting up the table."

A few minutes later I served the apéritif. I'd been drunk the night before, but it was unhealthy to go off booze cold turkey. When we ate afterward, Biki had a ferocious appetite.

Then the stars came out in the lazy night sky. The weather was going to be good the next day. When I lit the lantern, I had the feeling that we were on an island lost in space, amid unbelievable silence.

From his battered beach bag Biki pulled a few sticks of wood, old newspaper, two glasses, a tin teapot. He began brewing tea Arab-style. The steaming liquid went splashing into the glasses; then he broke the sugar by striking two lumps together. In that immense blackness these sounds sent a shiver of pleasure down my spine.

"How about you, Bert? What are you doing with your life?"

"Hell, I've had so many ups and downs that it feels like I'm on a fuckin' elevator."

"Where do you live?"

"In Nice."

"Well, I'm never going back to Europe. Except maybe to buy guns or get money for my Tuareg friends."

He spent a good part of the night talking to me about Tuaregs, Reguibats, Moors, and Toubous.

He seemed entirely committed to their cause.

According to him, an independence designed by some idiot diplomats had stripped those tribes of their Saharan motherland. They'd been sold out to the blacks of Mali, or those of Niger or Chad, all of whom were armed and advised by my froggy countrymen. The black infantry had massacred those nomads. In addition, the blacks had enacted highly prejudicial laws: any Targui who refused to give his daughter to a black could be fined and sent to jail.

The less-desirable nomads were disappearing little by little, forgetting their racial identity and leaving to mingle with their former slaves.

"In a way, maybe it isn't all that bad," he added, puffing on cigar number fifty. "They're just cleansing themselves of the sin of intermarriage. The big tents won't die out. The blacks like their pleasure too much. They sing, fuck, get drunk, and stuff themselves with food. They aren't capable of dying for an ideal. But the Targuis love death.

"You know, I'm so scared of being taken for a white nigger that once I tore up my papers. For two years now, I've been going around without an official identity. When I need papers, I either steal them or forge them. In any case, the cops are black. They take me for a Targui and haven't got the nerve to ask me for anything."

At dawn, after coffee, I gave him my P-38 automatic and a few clips of ammo for his friends. I also handed him some provisions for himself. Then we went our separate ways. He'd told me that he would write to me to keep in touch. And he did just that. I knew exactly how to reach him.

A heist like mine was tailor-made for a guy like him.

CHAPTER 9

The Lord Won't Give His Blessing

IN A VILLA overlooking the Mediterranean, the whole gang from Marseille stood stiffly at attention around an old man. I was there, too. Pierre had asked me to come. Before giving me his final word, he had to get the blessing of the "Lord."

The Lord was an old man. The godfather of everybody and his brother in the Nice underworld. Here, the great blue sea and the sun were all the baptismal font they needed.

He presided over the meal, eating little but talking a lot about the good old days, about a cabin at the back of a deep creek where he and his friends used to dance the Marseillaise waltz between two gang fights.

After the meal, we gathered on the living room veranda upstairs. Having come for the godfather's blessing, Pierre explained the job with an enthusiasm and an eloquence that could come only from a Marseillais. He made a heist through the sewers sound like some kind of opera. The old man listened in silence. He'd made so few mistakes in life that everyone relied on him like some kind of traffic cop at a busy intersection.

He said nothing, so we thought we had his blessing in the bag. Pierre sat down. All eyes on the venerable old man, we waited for the verdict.

Finally, he decided to put an end to our misery by shaking his head. Then, scratching his nose, the godfather explained his position.

What troubled him were possible repercussions for the Nice underworld. The size of this traditionally European under-world — the meanest, nastiest of them all — had swollen with the massive influx of *pieds-noirs.* You couldn't kid around with the guys from la Strunga and le Moucala. Since '62 they'd been warming their coffee with sticks of dynamite and scratching their behinds with pistol barrels. The old man felt that the job would start all kinds of trouble. Not to mention the cops, who were sure to declare war after a heist of these dimensions. Because the police had experienced political war to some extent and were beginning to learn how to use hostages. And the old man, becoming more disenchanted each second, went on scratching the wart he had on one nostril.

"All right, I know there are risks," Pierre persisted, "but that's only natural. We're talking about a haul of thirty to forty million francs. We can . . ."

The *consiglieri* raised both hands. "We've managed to carry out our business without you for generations. I say the job is too big for this town. If you don't understand that, your heads must be full of olive oil!"

And the old crook cut the conversation short. He didn't want to know anything. Yet this same man had burglarized churches; he'd fought over the honor of his women, over his reputation. He didn't know the word "fear." But our heist — he didn't even want to hear about it. He'd been in on that big train robbery, the Combinatie job. Just about everyone had been killed on that one. Yet this old man was still going strong and, from what people said, ready to start pulling jobs again. But when we asked him to give his blessing for our heist

— nothing doing. This all came as a hard blow for Pierre and his gang. Being from Marseille, they were on foreign territory in Nice. And their intrusion could lead to war.

So the boys from Marseille were angry. They'd fallen in love with the job. Especially Pierre. It was obvious that he wanted in at any cost. He looked twice as sore as the others.

You know what it's like when you're mad — you start nit-picking. The very next day they called to say that there was a meeting. They sent somebody to pick me up. A heist like that, they said, was just too good to be true. In fact, it couldn't be done. What the hell! Who ever heard of a bank with no seismic or ultrasonic alarm, no TV monitoring system? Why don't they just leave the key under the doormat while they're at it? It just couldn't be possible. Everyone knows a heist like that couldn't happen — not on this planet, at any rate.

"Yes, it *can* happen!" I protested. "The same company owns exactly the type of bank buildings in other towns, and they don't have any alarm, either. This info has been confirmed by somebody who's cased millions of jobs."

They looked flabbergasted. Actually, all they needed was a little reassurance. I used the momentum I'd gathered.

"As far as the haul is concerned, I can quote figures published by the bank itself. And according to those figures, the Nice branch (I still hadn't told them that we were going after the Société Générale) must have three or four times more money than that other bank I mentioned. In other words, thirty to forty million without counting nonnegotiable bank certificates, stocks and bonds, et cetera."

Sure, we heard that before. It's easy to pull a job — on paper. Theories — that's a lot of hot air. What's more, Bert Spaggiari is unknown in the underworld.

They really let me have it. I stood near the window, puffing

on a stogy. After a while le Vieux spoke in my defense. "Now
wait a minute. Bert knows So-and-so."

"That doesn't mean anything — we've never actually *worked*
together."

"And he's known So-and-so for a long time. They grew
up . . ."

"Nobody in jail thought too much of the political prisoners
who were doing time."

There I was, giving them the break of their lives, and they
weren't satisfied. They wanted me to hand them the son-of-a-
bitching money on a fuckin' silver platter. Well, they'd have to
count me out on that. If I'd offered them some miserable little
filling station holdup, they wouldn't have said a peep. But I
didn't care about their stupid yapping. Let them get it out of
their systems. They'd feel better afterward.

I didn't put up any resistance, so they gradually wore themselves out and it was all settled. Well, when I say "all settled,"
I mean relatively speaking. After days and days of yammering,
I managed to get a kind of halfway agreement — with one
clause: "If you're wrong about this job, we do a stretch in
prison. But do you know what you stand to get?"

Pierre said that with his teeth, not his tongue, as though he
were chewing me up already.

"You mean you rub me out, right?"

"I'm giving you till six this evening to be a hundred percent
certain of the story you're trying to sell us. Otherwise, just don't
come back. Because if it turns out that you're taking us for some
kind of ride, we'll break your goddamned back."

He said that in front of the others. It was like a contract,
signed, sealed, and delivered. I haven't the foggiest idea why he
did that. Up to then I'd been convinced that he trusted the plan
— and me. Except he had to bear the responsibilities. He was

bearing them, all right; only if the heist failed, it would be my neck.

Actually, he was for the job, the rest against. Some more so than others. The godfather had really put a scare into them.

For Pierre, the heist represented the long-awaited moment to assemble a team that had taken him years to screen. He was in no mood to miss this opportunity. Too many jobs had gone sour in recent months. At all costs he needed a good one to keep his reputation. In the underworld, social status becomes a matter of life or death. You've got to protect yourself against the younger generation, right? Furthermore, I was certain of one thing: no matter what his boys thought, no matter what the *consiglieri* told them, they all relied on Pierre. That was as plain as day. If he said yes, they'd all go along without hesitation.

It was getting on toward mid-April then. Outside, rain was falling. A drizzle that shrouded the hillside in mist. It must have been close to noon. La Fouine had just brought in sandwiches. I moved away from the window and went closer to the table. I toyed with a handful of change in my pocket while watching the boys.

"I don't need to wait until any damned six o'clock," I said coolly. "I stand by every claim I've made about the haul and the alarms."

I was going for broke. Actually, nobody was expecting me to back down. They looked at me in silence. There was a vacant look in their eyes, as though I'd just volunteered for a suicide mission, as though I were a dead man already. But that was only my personal impression.

Pierre came toward me with a big smile. He hugged me. Crooks, political prisoners, or adventurers, they all have that same spontaneous overflowing of sentiment.

"This calls for goddamned champagne!" exclaimed le Vieux from Castapiagne.

"Get out three bottles," Bouche d'or sang out.

And the whole gang came over to hug me. Then the celebration began.

Pierre still hadn't said yes, but everybody considered it as good as done. I was damned happy. Especially after the third glass of champagne. Relaxed, confident. Well, on the outside at least.

Till the very last day I was wondering what kind of knife they'd use to cut my throat. There was also the possibility of a dirty trick at the last moment. The possibility of being rubbed out, plain and simple. The possibility of losing my share of the loot. Anything could happen. That was why I needed friends. Real ones, my own kind. I didn't want any goddamned gang-war pros; I wanted soldiers, plain and simple.

When we split up at 3:00 A.M., I had half a load on. The atmosphere seemed to be closer to "agreed" than "maybe." But still nothing definite.

Two days later, I was driving back to Nice to buy some corn for my chickens. (I tried to do some poultry-raising, like an idiot. I'd made this decision with Audi after turning the photo store over to my manager.) I was coming back from the feed store near the waterfront. I'd just left the quai Cassini and was heading the Land Rover for the place Guynemer when a Peugeot delivery truck cut me off, forcing me up onto the sidewalk. A guy jumped out and rushed up to me, waving a piece of paper like it was a dispatch from the front.

It was the owner of the variety store next door to my place. He served as my mailbag.

"I spotted your jeep, Monsieur Bert. They just delivered a telegram at the store. It's addressed to Clément Hourrault, just like you said to watch for."

The telegram was from Sixty-eight. He would be coming to Nice in two days. All at once, I felt much stronger with an ally. I wasn't going to be alone anymore.

It was 10:00 A.M. The sun had come out, erasing the memory of the previous day's gloom. I drove downtown. After cruising around for ten minutes, I managed to find a parking spot — right on a pedestrian crosswalk. I left the car and went into a café to get change, not to drink coffee.

Then I went looking for a phone booth so that I could call the guy who was going to be the sixth member of my unit. His name was Gigi. He'd given me a phone number that actually belonged to the proprietress of a grocery store. She, in turn, relayed the message to the proprietress of the hotel where Gigi stayed. (The woman grocer explained that the relaying had to be done by one of her customers, for she wasn't on speaking terms with the hotel keeper.) The messenger came back to say that Gigi was at the café. "Which café?" I asked. The customer went back to find out. Fortunately, I'd gotten lots of change for the phone.

With Gigi, nothing could be simple. Luigi, alias Gigi, was an ex-paratrooper, an ex-mercenary. War had messed up his mind. He was really just a kid, a good fifteen years younger than I, and this was already his second try at adapting to civilian life. He was broke and just hanging around, waiting for something.

Physically, Gigi wasn't much to look at. But he was always ready to go for broke, anywhere, any time. What was more, he usually had an ace up his sleeve.

Sixty-eight, Rico, Carlos, Biki, Gigi. I still needed one more. I had two boys in mind but wanted to wait for Sixty-eight so that we could talk it over.

Two days later, on one of those sunny afternoons so common in Nice, Sixty-eight showed up at the appointed place with a canvas tote bag. We didn't say anything right away. We shook hands; nothing more. There was a bench nearby. He sat down. I leaned against the parapet separating the road from the beach. I pulled out a cigar. He smoked a cigarette. We smiled at each other. I'd known him for eight years. The old fire wasn't gleaming in his eyes anymore. Now they were dull, vacant. Time had sapped his enthusiasm and replaced it with something else — *nothing*.

They were the eyes of a man who knew you had to pay to get what you want. And just how expensive that could be.

CHAPTER 10

The First Trip into the Sewers

Wednesday, April 7, 11:30 A.M., Café de la Gare

"Paging Monsieur Armand. Phone call for Monsieur Armand."

I got up. Monsieur Armand was me. A code I'd set up with Pierre. I made my way to the phone booth. It was none too soon. I'd been coming in to drink my apéritif at that café for six days. Even Sixty-eight was starting to give me funny looks.

"Hello, Armand speaking."

"Today at three o'clock, same place."

"I'll be there."

Jesus Christ, why didn't he shit or get off the pot?

So Pierre had arrived in Nice with le Vieux from Castapiagne. I'd go to the meeting alone. This time the mood was tense, restless. I knew right away that they'd brought me an affirmative answer. Nobody is lighthearted about going into a heist. No more than a jealous husband going after his wife's lover or an infantryman about to assault an enemy position.

Pierre came to the door. We shook hands. "The answer is yes," he whispered.

"Are you sure?" I asked.

Ignoring my sarcasm, he continued:

"Tomorrow night we'll have a Four-L van just like the ones used by the highway department. Uniforms, hip boots, warning lights, and road barriers — we've got everything. We're going to pick you up downstairs in a blue Citroën. That's where we'll change our clothes. Then le Vieux will drive us to the Société Générale branch on the avenue Jean-Médecin. That's where we've got to go, right?"

Yes, that was it, all right.

"How did you know which bank it was?"

"It didn't take a mind reader to figure that out. Not with all the details you gave us." He spread his hands on the table and added, "You see? Everything is working out all right."

He meant, We could have pulled the job without you.

"Yesterday and the day before I sent people to 'your' bank," he continued. "I wanted to look things over before seeing your plans, before making up my mind."

Now he meant, I sent two or three guys to rent safe-deposit boxes and make sure you weren't telling us a bunch of lies.

"What was the verdict?" I asked.

"Everything seems to be in line with your description."

Le Vieux was already getting out the bottle of anisette. I got to my feet.

"Tomorrow night at seven P.M., downstairs. I'll come with the plans — and a pal. Better have an extra uniform."

"What size?"

"Same as yours."

Le Vieux stopped handing out glasses. The room became silent. I stuck a cigar in my mouth, then began pacing up and down. All you could hear was the creaking of the wooden floor under my soles.

"I'll be seeing you," I said, reaching the door. Then I took off.

The meeting had been rather chilly, if not actually icy. That was only to be expected. We'd gone from daydreams to reality.

The next day, at the scheduled time, a highway department van, followed by a light Citroën delivery truck, parked at the appointed spot. Pierre and le Vieux were waiting for us in the Citroën. From the outside it looked like an ordinary truck with the kind of round ventilator on the roof like they have on vehicles that carry perishable foods. Actually, it was set up like a trailer inside.

I handed Pierre the plans and introduced Sixty-eight. The two men from Marseille immediately focused their attention on him. Casually, Sixty-eight sat down. He didn't seem to give a flying fuck about their opinions. Sixty-eight was one cool customer. He must have done more sweating in those last five years than most criminals do in a lifetime. It showed on his face. Crooks have a sixth sense when it comes to judging a man. There was just no way you could be mistaken about that son of a bitch. This first specimen gave them an idea of what the rest of my men would look like. Not just tough — steel-plated.

We had lots of time on our hands, so Pierre glanced at the plans I'd brought. Le Vieux moved next to him, for he could also give an expert opinion. I was all ears.

"At a glance," began the leader of the Marseille gang, "these plans of yours tally perfectly with the information I've received. The distances and the layout do match our data. You know, with a little luck, there may not be any reinforced-concrete sheathing on the outer wall . . . it's so damn thick."

He was just kidding himself on that score, but it seemed pointless to argue the question. At the moment, I had something else on my mind. "Have you noticed the thickness of the strongbox doors?" I asked.

"Don't worry. With a blowtorch and a crowbar, we'll get through."

I didn't put any faith in the torch and crowbar. But he was a specialist and more competent than I in that area. And after all, wasn't that the very reason I'd taken him for a partner?

But I just didn't like the blowtorch and crowbar. "Look, there's still time to get flatirons made," I suggested.

He shrugged.

All right, I ought to rely on him. I dropped the subject. I was wrong.

The "flatiron" is a burglar's tool that's as old as the hills. It offers the double advantage of being quick and noiseless. It's actually a steel I-beam cut to the width of the safe. You prop the beam against the inner edge of the enormous safe doors. Then a hydraulic jack resting inside the I-beam thrusts against the individual doors of the boxes, ripping them off their hinges.

Crack three thousand safe-deposit boxes with a blowtorch? I just couldn't swallow that.

8:00 P.M., the same day

The highway department van turned down the avenue Félix-Faure. Le Vieux was at the wheel. Pierre sat beside him. Sixty-eight and I were in the back seat with the equipment. Except for the driver, who wore no wading boots, we were all dressed like sewer workers.

On the place Masséna, the light truck went careening around the corner of the rue Gioffrédo. "Jesus! Take it easy on the turns! We don't have any seat belts back here!" I was the one who yelled that. I was getting sore.

First of all, le Vieux drove too goddamned fast. Second, I doubted that sewer specialists rode around four in a truck. That just wasn't professional. We were taking unnecessary chances. From here on, I was going to demand that decisions be made jointly. Better yet, I'd do all the deciding myself.

That's what I was thinking as we drove down the rue Saint-Michel. A few seconds later, the vehicle stopped outside the bank, at the corner of rue de l'Hôtel-des-Postes and the rue Deloye. Our manhole was located on the rue Deloye.

My watch showed 9:45 P.M. Traffic was still fairly heavy on the avenue Jean-Médecin, but where we were, you couldn't see a soul. Fortunately, the rue Deloye was narrow, with the manhole located smack in the middle of the street.

Le Vieux jumped out of the van, waving a red flag. I could imagine what would have happened if there'd been lots of traffic. Sixty-eight got out of the back to set up the road markers and a MEN WORKING sign. As for Pierre, he stuck the crowbar in the middle of the manhole cover and swung it off. I gave him a hand dragging the steel cover clear of the hole. When that was done, he dropped the crowbar and began climbing down. I went rushing to the van for the three lanterns. Then came Sixty-eight's turn to go underground. I was just about to follow him when I spotted a bus full of cops coming our way down the rue Saint-Michel.

Le Vieux hadn't seen them. He was watching the other way. We were really getting off to a great start! Anyway, I tried to look busy at the back of the truck. I pulled out a toolbox. I started to diddle around with some washers. The bus pulled up. Exactly four yards away from me. Jesus Christ! Le Vieux finally saw it.

I thought he was going to walk straight over to the police bus. No, his first instinct was to stay put; then, prompted no doubt by his senility, he burst out laughing. The chuckle became a guffaw and, finally, a regular fit of laughing.

Three cops got out of the bus, staring at this crazy old fart who clung to his MEN WORKING sign to keep his balance during this laughing spell. What a way to pull a job!

Nighttime. I'm sorting out gaskets in the street next to a manhole, in front of a bank. The cops arrive just as my partner, a hardened criminal, hand-picked for the heist of the century, decides to start a riot.

One of the three cops was a sergeant. "Still working?" he asked, looking at me suspiciously. "Never a dull moment, eh? What's the matter — how come we weren't told?"

I threw the box down the pavement.

"That's right. Just what you said — 'Still working'! But look what they give me to work with! This old fart is laughing because I took out the wrong box! Well, just go right on laughing, pal! They're not getting me back on the same truck with you. Tomorrow I'm going to see Perrault; you can bet your fuckin' ass on that."

"Come on, boys. No sense fighting. You're both working for the same boss," the sergeant said, stepping between us.

Behind me, one of the cops blew his whistle. Two cars wanted to mount the curb to get around the bus. The policeman made them back up while the driver of the bus cleared the way. Meanwhile, the sergeant leaned over the edge of the manhole, looking down. That was when Pierre decided to yell, "Well, where the hell is that goddamned washer?"

An odd expression came over his face when he saw the policeman's cap.

The bus finally left. The cops went away because they'd received a message over the radio. A brawl had erupted outside a movie theater or something like that. Le Vieux apologized for leaving me in the lurch. But he was really tickled pink. He saw a good omen in the fact that things had gone wrong at the start. Lady Luck was winking at us, he maintained. Everything that happened, from the beginning to the end of this job, was some kind of omen.

Now I went down the ladder. In a few seconds, le Vieux would pull the cover back over the manhole, pack up our equipment, and drive off. He would come to get us at five o'clock the next morning.

The tunnel I'd landed in was four feet high and three feet across. Sewage coated the walls. I could feel the filthy muck in my hair already. No sooner did Pierre hand me down my lantern than the manhole cover slid shut over our heads. We were cut off from the world. From here on, the stench of sewage would stay in our nostrils.

The beams of our flashlights cut through the darkness, il-luminating slimy ghosts, while monstrous oozings hung from the vaulted brick ceiling. Groping ahead, we felt that at any second we might step over the edge of a deep well. We moved through the muck, our shoulders stooped, half-expecting the tentacles of an octopus to come slithering around our necks.

We might get lost, I thought as our rubber hip boots made sucking noises in the filth. What if we went sliding into some cesspool? Wheezing, panting, we groped our way. The idea was to locate all the tunnels that touched the bank. But what if somebody decided to park a truck over our manhole cover and we couldn't get back out? Every now and then, we stopped to listen to gurglings, muffled rumblings that emanated from the bowels of the earth.

"Jesus Christ, there'd better be enough air in this goddamned hole!" Sixty-eight remarked.

Not enough air. That idea has haunted me all my life, ever since I watched a funeral go by when I was five.

"What did he die of?" I asked an old neighbor.

"That idiot must have forgotten to breathe."

"People really die from that?"

"Certainly they do!"

From that day on, I'd always watched my breathing. I was even afraid to sleep, for fear that I wouldn't have enough oxygen and would start choking.

Later on, much later, this fear became a reality when I tried scuba diving with "air tanks" of my own manufacture. And here I was, back together with my old terror, almost as if we'd made an appointment.

In the weeks to come, this dull anguish often gripped me. It would become excruciating for an instant, like a tender scar that you touch by accident.

We combed that sector of the sewer system until two or three in the morning. From time to time we'd come to a spot where it was too low to stand. Then we'd stop for a smoke, exchange a smile, or just look at our own reflection in the other guy's filth-streaked face. Then we'd start on our way again. We counted our steps. Each man kept count of his own. Afterward, we would average them up, then compare the distances with landmarks on the street. In this way, we worked out a map of that Swiss cheese.

"Quit counting out loud, damn it! You're getting me all mixed up! Now where the fuck was I?"

"Do you mean before or after you started talking? Fifty-nine."

"What about you?"

"I've got forty-four."

"What happened? Did you slip, or is that your age?"

Eventually we even forgot the hideous stench. We grew so accustomed to the sewer that we would rinse the muck off our hands under the streams of urine that came pouring from nearby toilets at odd intervals.

It was almost 5:00 A.M. by Pierre's watch, which he claimed was waterproof. At any rate, it must have been solid, because there was some crap stuck to the large hand.

We came back to the manhole under the rue Deloye.

"Do you see this spot?" I asked, showing Pierre a section of wall located two or three steps from the manhole shaft.

"What about it?"

"This is where we dig."

"How do you know?"

"You can see for yourself on the maps. According to my calculations, the middle of the vault should lie along this line."

"Now he tells me — after we spend the whole night in this shithouse!"

"You had to come with us to see the route markers. You've got to understand where you're going to be working. We'll be in the sewer for days, even weeks."

"Why not say 'years'? I don't need to spend the whole son-of-a-bitching night here to understand that. And what the hell is the sense of all this surveying if you already know where to dig?"

It was Sixty-eight who answered. "Now that the markers have been set up and our surveying is done, we can settle down to finding means of access. You've got to know this part of the city sewers like the palm of your hand. That's the best insurance policy you can have in case we run into cops."

"Now you understand why we can't bring in men or equipment through this manhole," I added. "It would be too dangerous."

"Of course. You've got to enter the sewers someplace where there's no one around."

"And leave ourselves a way out in case of trouble. I'll work on that tomorrow night with Sixty-eight."

Pierre buried his hand absently in the muck adhering to the wall.

"It can't be more than twelve or fifteen inches thick," he said. "After that . . ."

"After that, it's easy as pie. A mixture of earth and stones like you find all over this part of the country. Then you're at the wall of the vault. After that, we're on Easy Street!"

Pierre looked first at me, then at Sixty-eight. After that, he looked at the wall again. He wore the expression of a man who hasn't forgotten a single detail.

"A few yards behind this crap is paradise," he murmured.

Then he aimed a punch at the wall to see if it was solid or not. The filth splattered everywhere.

CHAPTER 11

Voyage to the Anus of the Earth

Friday, April 9

We spent part of the afternoon walking in the streets around the bank. We were trying to see if the survey we'd made the night before agreed with the street-level layout. We checked it off on an enlarged map of the neighborhood.

Pierre and le Vieux, satisfied with the results of this first stage, headed back for Marseille that night. Their mission: to procure the necessary equipment and begin the operation as soon as it had been found.

For me and Sixty-eight, it was quite another story. We were going to spend the whole weekend and a good part of the following week messing around in the underground town. We'd decided to sleep days. At night, we would go in through the anus of the city and mark out its bowels until 3:00 A.M. or so. For my own peace of mind, I told my wife that I was driving up to Paris to attend a series of political meetings.

The objective, for Sixty-eight and me, was to locate a nice, quiet manhole. After that, we had to map a route leading from there to the bank. But without losing sight of the fact that several tons of equipment would need to be carried to the work site. And that we also had to allow for the possibility of a hasty retreat.

Saturday night, April 10

We decided to go under the city where the Paillon River comes out at the Mediterranean.

The Paillon is a little river that runs down from the top of the Savel and from Mont Ours, having its mouth at the Bay of Angels some fifteen miles below. A large stretch of the river, which runs through downtown Nice, has been roofed with concrete. So, wending its way under the city streets, the Paillon is linked indirectly with the sewer system.

The river's broad, shallow mouth runs under the Promenade des Anglais, disappearing on the beach opposite the theater, not far from the Hôtel Méridian. In other words, there's nothing particularly secluded about the place, especially in good weather. And sure enough, that Saturday night the weather was beautiful. Couples, hippies, tourists — everybody was out. We had to wait until 1:00 A.M. before we could get into the concrete conduit of the Paillon without being seen.

The conduit, made up of four archways, was cavernous. In fact, we instinctively hugged the walls every time a train rumbled overhead at high speed. We learned afterward that the conduit stayed cavernous throughout its course under the city, to carry off huge volumes of water after a heavy rain, no doubt.

That night we found a sewer entrance that would take us right under the rue de France. But not without problems. At one point we were nearly carried away by an avalanche of sewage that filled our hip boots with filthy muck. Then, after losing our way several times, we managed to get back to the Paillon River around 7:00 A.M.

We returned to the mouth of the river and the beach. Exhausted, shivering with cold, permeated through and through by sewage, we had no choice but to strip to our underpants and swim in the freezing Mediterranean while a bunch of amused vacationers watched us through binoculars.

On Sunday we went underground separately as soon as night fell. We were lucky: the temperature had dropped, so there wasn't a soul around. The town had practically ceased to exist.

We dropped our huge packs in the shadows under the archways and changed into our uniforms. Taking balls of string, knives, compasses, electric lanterns, we plunged ahead into the darkness.

This time we went much farther up the Paillon, returning to a vast sewer under the avenue Jean-Médecin that we'd only glimpsed the night before. On either side of that underground avenue lay dozens of ducts. We went up one that seemed to lead under the bank but which, after a few hundred yards, ran into a dead end. It was blocked up with concrete. We tried other tunnels that also led nowhere.

We couldn't find our way back to the sewers we'd explored with Pierre the first night. Fortunately, we had the compasses and our balls of string. The sewers form a kind of maze, a chaotic anthill of ducts, tunnels, and culverts. I haven't mentioned the rats — we'll see about them later. We were nowhere near the anus of that cesspool.

At about 2:00 A.M. we found the second entrance of the Félix-Faure sewer. We'd found the first one, too narrow for easy access, early that night.

It was an opening placed up high on the sewer wall, overlooking a sluice gate that we had to climb to reach a platform protected by a railing. At the end stood a steel door and, behind it, an outlet for electrical power. Sixty-eight and I traded glances. We both had the same idea — that power source was a windfall. It belonged to the underground garage that was being built beneath a huge square, the place Masséna.

We decided to return the next day to take a wax impression of the lock, from which we'd pattern a key for later on. We topped off the night by scouting a sizable culvert — five feet high — under the northern sidewalk of the avenue Félix-Faure.

Monday night, same program. It had rained, but the course of the Paillon River had scarcely changed — sewers included. The same number of holes, the same muck and slime, the same pipes vomiting filth unexpectedly.

Things went faster that night. And we finally got back to the markers left the first day with Pierre. We'd made the link-up. On the right, at the end of the Félix-Faure culvert, a duct three feet in diameter emptied into the Paillon. To the left was a culvert five feet by two — the Chauvain main sewer.

About one hundred and fifty yards from there, on the left, an oval manhole ran beneath the rue Gioffrédo — six feet high by two feet wide at shoulder height. We sloshed ahead another hundred and fifty yards through a foot of liquid filth. What's more, the walls of the tunnel seemed coated with excrement, as if the stuff had been sprayed on with a firehose. Finally, to the right, we saw the conduit that would link us up to the rue Deloye.

We went over the route four times to get used to it and to draw permanent markers. Afterward, we set out to look for new ways of reaching the street.

Sometime on Tuesday night or Wednesday morning, about a mile after the Chauvain main sewer, we came across a sluice gate on the Paillon and a trap door opening on a construction site. From here we could see an Arab café across the street — L'Aube de l'Islam, The Dawn of Islam. We'd come out on the quai Saint-Jean.

I had to laugh, seeing that café! I remembered one of those
nights long ago when three different teams had received the
same order: blow up the Mercier pharmacy. It was a dispute
over money between a rich drug-store owner and some shady
character. The first team had done its work. But the other two
teams looked like idiots, standing there with their little bundles
in front of the wreckage of the pharmacy. And one after another, without consulting each other, they set their dynamite in
front of the Café L'Aube de l'Islam. That wasn't the first time
that the OAS had gotten rid of a package in front of that café.
We all laugh about it today. But I guess it's you, Mohammed,
who had the last laugh.

So Sixty-eight and I found the ideal opening. The Café
L'Aube de l'Islam was located halfway between the place Masséna and the Palais des Expositions. I could see only one drawback — actually, fairly minor compared with the advantages of
the location. The hole was quite a long way from the bank
— let's say, about a mile or a mile and a half via the sewers. We
nevertheless put off exploring it until Wednesday night, in case
we found a more convenient entrance.

And we did find one. It was a passageway located in the
courtyard of a building. One hitch: right next door stood a
bank. The entrance was a kind of spill gate, covered only with
rusty sheet metal; it led to the Gioffrédo sewer. We could easily
park our truck over the trap door, then lower ourselves into the
sewer with all the equipment through a hole cut in the floor of
the truck. We'd have to see about that. It was complicated
— a bank, the courtyard of a building, the problem of maneuv-
ering a trailer truck . . .

At any rate: mission accomplished.

Thursday, April 15

Sixty-eight finally took possession of the apartment I'd told him to lease. We would house the gang there.

It was a five-room, furnished apartment with a balcony. Most important, it had two entrances, one of them through the garage. Sixty-eight had rented it under a false name, of course. Eight thousand francs in advance.

In the apartment, we worked out the final details. First of all, there was a map of the route (the Café L'Aube de l'Islam to the bank), which was prepared in several copies and handed out to the boys from Marseille. Then we made up the list of earth-moving equipment we'd need to dig the tunnel — wood for shorings, hemp baskets for the debris. I didn't know if Pierre had put those items on his list or if I should take charge of them.

We also had to be ready for the arrival of other members of the unit. Extra beds and linens had to be provided.

With regard to the seventh member of our team, Sixty-eight had recommended one of his close friends. Built like a tank, Mick was a tremendous blacksmith. In addition, Sixty-eight claimed that he'd bring us good luck. Mick was the fellow who'd rescued Sixty-eight from the Iraqi border guards, carrying him piggyback through more than one hundred miles of mountainous country.

That night, to celebrate the completion of our survey of the sewer route, Sixty-eight and I treated ourselves to a huge feed. During the meal, I asked him what he planned to do with his share. He was evasive. Talking about that kind of thing didn't interest him.

"I don't have any plans," he answered.

A few years before, he would have said, "I'm going to get together all those friends of mine and build the inn we've been dreaming about." He'd been crazy about that idea once.

Since then, he had lost some friends and a good many illusions. He'd given up on all that — politics, friends, old dreams. Those things were over.

CHAPTER 12

The Arrival of the Unit and Waiting for D-Day

Saturday, April 17

Across the way from The Wild Geese, the sun had come up over Villeplaine. It played over the treetops and filtered through the thickest brambles. It warmed the tiles still wet with the dew while casting the mountain's gigantic shadow over the plain.

Audi had dragged me out of bed; she wanted a rabbit for the polenta. She knew that I had my best chances of bagging one at dawn. The next day would be Easter.

I took my shotgun down from the wall, shoveled a handful of shells into my pocket, and walked outside to finish my coffee. My big Dobermans were already frisking about. As a rule, they didn't stir before 10:00 A.M. Not even to give the first person up and about a little lick. But as soon as they caught the scent of gunpowder, they went wild. Especially Parka, the older one. She pretended to bark, simulated a sprint start, then came racing back to me.

Though born and raised in an apartment, the dogs understood shotguns, mountain trails — and cats. Somewhere, Parka must have met a hunting dog that had told her about these things. And she must have taught Vespa. What other explanation could there be?

When I get to some impassable ledge in the mountains, I tell her, "Find me a path, Parka!" And off she goes, looking — and, sure enough, she finds it. Once, when we were away for a vacation at an old farm in the Alps, she saw shepherd dogs leading a flock of sheep. By the fourth day, she was sorting out the lambs, pushing the goats to one side, harassing the stragglers. She was doing work that takes the pros six months to learn.

Audi appeared in the doorway, ready to leave for her Saturday morning job. She was always gorgeous in the morning. I set down my coffee and went over to kiss her. Afterward, I walked her out to the car. I knew what I'd have to tell her that night: I was going to attend another meeting in Paris, one that would last longer than the first. I hated lying to her. And maybe I didn't really want to go away . . . I don't know. In the breast of every adventurer lies a homebody, a TV watcher.

When I gave her another kiss, she clung to me as though she suspected something.

"So long. I've got to go now or I'll miss those rabbits again." I broke away and headed for the vast field of alfalfa.

I'd spent the better part of my life on the run. Trying to dance to the rhythm of some damned music that didn't even exist. The world was still out there, waiting to be conquered. There were kingdoms, empires waiting to be built . . . but it wasn't 6:00 A.M. yet, and I had to go hunting for rabbits.

In a few days, in a few weeks, I was going to be able to help people who needed it. But what about me? Who would help me?

Not so long before, I'd said, "When I get some money, I'll do this and that." I'd been planning to plant trees, have the road improved, install electricity, build a chalet for some friends, a little pool for Parka. Time had gone by and, with it, all my good resolutions. In just a few days, in a few weeks at most, I'd be a rich man, but still just as mixed up.

No child, no tribe. Maybe that's been my downfall — not having children. I could have built them a mountain stronghold, an eagle's roost from which they might plunder the valley below and make the mountain fertile. But we'd never had any.

And we won't have any now. It was too late. The tribe would be limited to an Adam and Eve, fruitless on a barren earth.

April of 1976 was coming to an end. Rico and Carlos arrived from Spain in a camper on April 24. Gigi had come in from Florence three days before. I'd gone to meet him at the station. There he was, lugging a huge cardboard suitcase. Gigi had three months to kill; then he'd be off to South Africa as a mercenary. He was just hoping to pick up a little money from the heist.

"Not too much, just a little. You can donate the rest to your favorite charity," he told me minutes after getting off the train. As a rule, it's always the greedy ones who say that. But Gigi was sincere — he proved it. He didn't give a damn about money.

Another guy who would volunteer his services for a good cause was Biki. He arrived on Monday, the 26th. Biki, the "Targui" man. His passport and car were Swiss. He'd brought a girl along. "A girl for the troops," he announced. Her name was Mireille. She was tall and dark-haired, with a voluptuous figure. How the hell did Biki manage to come up with a piece like that in two days? Any son of a bitch who trots in a gorgeous babe and announces, casually, "For the troops," has to be able to do anything.

You couldn't help liking Biki, because you knew right away this son of a bitch didn't give a damn if anybody liked him. Personally, I bawled him out. That was my job. "It's out of the question. She just can't live with us. Too damned risky having a broad around."

They all had to agree with me. But we ended up letting her stay. What the hell? We'd gotten her as a present. What were we supposed to do — send her to a goddamned hotel?

Mick had also arrived. Furthermore, he'd been the first to come. He was every inch the gorilla that Sixty-eight had described. He looked like he knew his way around.

I had a fine bunch of sandhogs and, in case of trouble, the best fighting unit ever put together in France.

We were living eight in a five-room apartment. To avoid arousing suspicion, only Sixty-eight and Mireille used the elevator. The rest of us took the freight elevator in the garage. The damned thing groaned under our weight. We got along. Everyone was nice and easygoing. At the beginning it was terrific. Then people started getting ants in their pants. It was already May, and Pierre hadn't gotten in touch with us.

The days went by. We waited. And we got sick and tired of waiting.

We didn't know that during this time the boys from Marseille were knocking themselves out trying to swipe the equipment we needed for the job. Cars, trucks, oxygen tanks, blowtorches, hydraulic jacks, and various other items. Later on, we realized that this must have been the most hazardous phase of the whole heist.

For example, they decided to "borrow" more than forty tanks of liquid oxygen from a warehouse. On their first try, the night watchman was fast asleep in a corner, hidden from view. He woke up all of a sudden and started yelling his damned head off. He ran around, hollering and throwing stones to give the alarm, while our boys were trying to tackle him. Finally, they had to make a run for it when the police came.

On their second try, they went to another warehouse and loaded forty-one tanks on their truck. Bam! The cops show up again. This time the poor bastards had to abandon the truck with its entire load.

Another time, a member of the Marseille bunch was stealing tools from a trailer truck parked outside a roadside diner. He got caught by one truck driver, and a whole bunch of the driver's friends came out. They left the poor guy for dead.

Another Marseillais got himself locked in a machine shop and had to spend the whole damned night there.

PART TWO

THE HEIST

CHAPTER 13

It's On for Tomorrow

"WHAT DO YOU SAY — are there alarms in that goddamned place or aren't there?"

Weren't they ever going to get off my back with that stupid crap?

"No, god damn it, there aren't any!"

"If there is one, we'll know about it even before we get through the wall," la Fouine said, positively.

Pierre got up from the sofa, where he'd been stretched out. He stopped to look at himself in the mirror.

"We'll check one more time," he said, jerking his thumb my way. "We'll send somebody in with that radio set of yours."

Le Tombeur suggested tossing a firecracker down the air vent. One of my own boys would never have come up with a moronic idea like that. I got to my feet and bit on my cigar to keep from screaming.

"Listen, a seismic alarm system goes off when there's a noise. It stops as soon as the noise stops. If you really want to run another check, I've got something better than a radio. I've put together a siren with a timer that operates on batteries."

I took a step toward Pierre.

"Put it in one of the safe-deposit boxes you rented and let's settle this business once and for all. I'll set the timer for any hour you want, and I guarantee the noise will be loud enough to go right through the vault. Besides, a seismic alarm goes off if you so much as whisper."

"All right. How long is this siren of yours set to blow?"

"Four minutes."

"Have you got it in your car?"

"Yes."

"Give it to me in a little while. One other thing — we don't have enough timbers for shoring up the tunnel. Can you see about that?"

"No sweat."

"What about your boys? I'd like to meet them. Everybody should get to know one another. Bring them around tomorrow at noon. There's lots of room here; we'll have a real feed." He stretched lazily and yawned, then walked over to the table for his cigarettes. "See the nice setup we have here? Not bad, eh?" He waved his arm, indicating the huge living room. Next, he ran his gaze over his men. They were all there. Bouche d'or and le Vieux were reading the same newspaper. La Fouine was shining his shoes. Mathieu and le Tombeur lay sprawled in armchairs. Hervé, the youngest, was playing solitaire. I puffed on a stogy, my elbows propped up on the sideboard at the back of the room.

"All things being equal, we start the day after tomorrow," Pierre announced. He was saying this more for his men than me.

I moved away from the sideboard and headed for the ashtray on the table. "Wait a minute," I interrupted. "Assuming the experiment with the siren goes right, we start tomorrow night."

This cast a chill over the atmosphere. It was the first time I'd ever locked horns with their leader. All eyes went from him to me, as if they were watching a tennis match.

Pierre made no move. He studied me through his cigarette smoke. He was a tough customer, that Pierre. The son of a bitch wasn't afraid of anything. And I'd challenged him. His silence proved that he had no intention of backing down. Neither did I.

Then le Vieux stepped in. "If his gang does the digging . . ." he said, gesturing my way.

"Yes, that's right," Bouche d'or chimed in, folding up his newspaper and getting to his feet. "If he wants to start tomorrow, that's his lookout." He looked at the others for support.

"It's up to Pierre," snapped le Tombeur, as though it was clear who'd won.

Pierre looked at Bouche d'or, then at his feet. After that, he went to the window. The one next to me. He gazed at the garden for a while. He was squinting like a man groping through the fog. Only it was a fine spring day.

"We'll see about that tomorrow," he said finally, almost without moving his lips. And he turned to his boys. His tanned face was lined with fatigue. "Jesus Christ, get out the bottle," Pierre added abruptly. "What with this heist and all, I almost forgot our apéritif."

Relieved, everyone laughed at this vague hint of humor.

The incident was ended, not settled. Neither side wanted to give ground. But by the same token, nobody was trying to aggravate the situation. Quite the contrary. People from Marseille just aren't like that.

Half an hour later, amid the clink of ice cubes, they were joking about their recent move. The way they told it, I split my sides laughing. Jeannot-Bouche d'or had been assigned the job of finding them a place. He'd contacted practically every real estate agent in the area. There was absolutely nothing to be had. Not a villa for twenty miles around. In desperation, he'd made up his mind to rent two furnished apartments and two garages in a nearby suburb.

Then, just the day before, Bouche d'or picked up some middle-aged broad. She took him up to her place. Middle-aged women were Bouche d'or's specialty. As long as he could remember, he'd always preferred older women. This particular one turned out to be the owner of a fabulous villa. According to Bouche d'or, it's common knowledge that guys who prefer older women are the greatest lovers. At any rate, for the modest sum of two hundred francs, he persuaded the broad to take her summer vacation a couple of months earlier than usual.

So the gang moved right into that mansion, which must have been built prior to World War I, but looked like it hadn't been repaired since the Franco-Prussian War. Whole patches of stucco had flaked off, revealing the red brick underneath. You should have seen the elegant old bathtubs. Almost all the plumbing was blocked up, but you could shower by means of a plastic tube connected to the faucet of the bathroom sink (which had to be propped up with orange crates). That's how the whole place was. Wallpaper coming down, electrical wiring secured with bent nails, chairlegs unglued. A decrepit mansion full of the dreams and silence of a bygone era.

Giant hedges seemed to insulate the mansion from the frenzy of this century. There was a date palm next to a broad staircase, on an Unter den Linden lane. A fig tree had grown right up through the floor of an old gazebo. Farther on, rose bushes had turned into brambles, and, beyond that, a whole damned jungle had overrun everything — right up to the old wash house, which was surrounded by an ivy-covered fence. I would have enjoyed strolling around there, looking for ghosts, but the Marseillais were beckoning to me.

Taking up the entire basement of the house, the garage was bursting with vehicles: a light Citroën delivery truck, a Volkswagen Kombi, a big Peugeot truck, and a brand-new Estafette loaded with equipment. The stuff had been plenty hard to come by.

The next day, when I went back to that garage, I had my team with me. Bouche d'or was monopolizing the attention of Gigi, a specialist who couldn't speak French very well. Le Vieux had taken Biki, the man of the desert; Mathieu had teamed up with Rico; le Tombeur was working with Mick. Each guy explained how his tools worked. They ran their hands over the equipment, murmuring words of affection, bragging about its potential.

I think that Pierre and his bunch warmed up immediately to the guys in my unit. Mine were close-mouthed; his couldn't stop talking. Mine were standoffish; his playful and outgoing. The differences must have attracted them to each other.

"Bravo, your boys look first-rate!" Pierre confided to me.

And then we went into the huge kitchen to eat. Le Vieux and Bouche d'or had been up since 6:00 A.M., preparing a meal in our honor. What was more, the siren had spent the night in a safe-deposit box without setting off an alarm. Morale was at an all-time high.

Carlos seemed to be the liveliest member of our unit. He massacred the French language even worse than Gigi; however, that never fazed him. He began talking over old times with three of the Marseillais. They had lived in Spain when all the French hoods started to immigrate there.

I didn't know Carlos like I knew Rico. Physically, he was fairly short, dark-skinned. He had a real lantern jaw and a thin, hooked nose. Carlos always wore a bandanna. Oddly enough, he was the one who most fascinated the Marseillais at that dinner. He'd been placed across from Pierre and every now and then, when they looked at each other, it reminded me of two bulls ready to lock horns.

Biki kept passing out cigarillos, as though he'd paid for the whole meal. And it wasn't long before he started cracking jokes that came straight from the Canebière in Marseille. He'd flown to Switzerland aboard an Air Africa jet, so . . .

"When you fly Air Africa, the first-class passengers eat the tourist-class passengers for lunch."

The boys from Marseille were in heaven.

The most unsociable member of the gang was Rico. He just plain refused to eat the ratatouille. We were on the verge of a diplomatic incident. As the person in charge, I hastily assured Bouche d'or and le Vieux that the stuff was delicious. Over and over, I praised the quality of this Marseillais specialty. And as I did, I kept kicking Rico under the table, trying to get him to apologize, to do something. But no — the son of a bitch wouldn't say a word. He just pushed his chair away from the table and got up.

Everybody stopped eating to watch him go striding into the kitchen. When he vanished, the gang from Marseille looked at each other, puzzled. I was just as puzzled as they were.

He came back a few seconds later armed with a goddamned sword that he must have taken down from over the fireplace. Once more, we all stopped eating. Rico went over to the sink and put the sword on the drain. Then, using a knife, he carved big chunks out of a roast beef. He walked out again. This time he came back with a lighted blowtorch. And that's how he roasted his meat, skewered on the sword.

"Let us try some of that!" the boys began to shout.

I'd been placed next to Mick. We'd only known each other for three weeks but we got along nicely. Something clicked right away between us. He'd started out in life as a salesman. But, like so many big, muscle-bound guys, he was rather shy. He just couldn't make a sale. One day, his superior called him into the office: "Get out there and just be yourself!"

It was the worst piece of advice he could have given him. Three days later, Mick got the sack.

After coffee, Pierre suggested a game of *pétanque*. The Marseillais bowled against us on the lawn until about 4:00 P.M. That was when I stood up and pulled a sheaf of papers out of my inside breast pocket. I placed them on the table.

"Three copies of the map showing our route through the sewers. Look them over, if you like."

"Nice work," Pierre murmured after studying one. Then he added, "Of course, that's a long way . . ."

"It's got to be long if we want safety. That's the only quiet manhole we found."

"All right," he said, getting to his feet. Bouche d'or did the same.

"What about that game of *pétanque?*" he asked.

I'd just pulled on my jacket.

"Sorry. We'll have to save that for some other time."

"What 'other time'? You must think that we'll have . . ."

Bouche d'or stopped when he saw my men gathering up their cigarettes and lighters and heading my way.

"We start tonight," I said casually.

Pierre nodded, looked at his shoes, then went back to the window, just as he'd done the morning before. He stared at the linden trees with the smug expression of a man who'd planted them himself. He kept staring at them. "All right," he said finally, still looking at the garden.

"You're right," he added a few seconds later, turning to me. I stuck out my hand and he shook it.

"Le Vieux will come and pick you up at ten o'clock tonight. Will that be all right?"

"Sure."

"One other thing — all of us are coming."

This was something I'd never expected.

Reaching the door, le Vieux said to me, "I'll come and pick you up in the big Peugeot truck. Do you think you can all fit in — what with the gear and everything? Do you want me . . ."

"We'll squeeze in somehow." Then, remembering the way he drove, I said, "Could you please try not to get a speeding ticket on the way over? We're in no special hurry."

CHAPTER 14

May 7 to May 8, 1976

Friday, May 7, 1976, 9:30 P.M.

We went over the gear in the apartment. Belts, canteens, sheath knives, wading boots, camouflage fatigues, packs, flashlights. Then there were the individual tools: a folding jimmy that I'd forged myself, entrenching tools, picks, and the rest.

Mireille was in the kitchen, whipping up our snacks. The unit gathered in the living room, some stretching out on the sofas, others sitting. A hush fell over the place. Each man knew his assignment; we'd talked it over dozens of times. We knew that it would be tough. In a few minutes we were going to take the plunge. We were ready.

11:00 P.M.

A gray Peugeot truck pulled up alongside the curb across from the Café L'Aube de l'Islam.

A man jumped out of the truck with two MEN WORKING signs. Another one, armed with a steel hook, raised a rectangular manhole cover. Now a third man emerged from the vehicle and disappeared into the sewer. Quickly, equipment passed from hand to hand. The stuff piled up at the bottom of the ladder: hydraulic jacks, bundles of lumber for shoring up tunnels, tools, hemp baskets for earth removal, cartons of Evian mineral water . . .

All of a sudden the guy standing near one of the MEN WORKING signs waved his arm. A few seconds later, a Volkswagen Kombi came rolling noiselessly to a stop behind the truck. Six men jumped out and, one by one, disappeared down the manhole.

The truck driver dragged the heavy cover back into place, folded up the road signs, then climbed into the cab of his vehicle and sped off.

Underground, in the wavering light of the lanterns, the human chain passed the gear through a twenty-yard maze of pipes and coffers until it lay in the dry bed of the Paillon River.

Now the men divided up part of the cargo without speaking. The long march began.

Within the first fifty yards, someone slipped and landed on his backside. Another man went skidding into the cold water. Those with the heaviest burdens shifted their loads to the other shoulder. The weaker men began looking for convenient rocks where they could sit and rest.

We still had a long way to go, half a mile or more. We were moving under one of the four archways that covered the underground course of the Paillon River. Now and then a man would play the beam of his flashlight on the vaulted concrete overhead. We were wading through nearly a foot of water, so the cavernous tunnel resounded with our splashing and floundering.

Every two hundred yards or so, wide gaps in the wall made it possible for us to reach the adjacent tunnels. Here and there we'd see an old air mattress or some blankets lying in one of those openings. This led us to suspect that the high-ceilinged tunnel served as a kind of flophouse for winos and hippies. I'd never noticed that on my explorations with Sixty-eight. It made me uneasy. But my fears proved unfounded.

The bed of the river must have been lined with cement once. Now, it was choked with gravel forming dams that trapped debris of all kinds: the carcasses of dead animals that had been carried downstream, rusting motorbikes, automobile tires, and even shopping carts from supermarkets.

Half an hour later, we had dropped our burdens on a low-lying island facing the culvert that led to the last tunnel. This gravel islet became our rest camp. The first advance base.

In better physical condition than the Marseillais, my men went back for the rest of the gear.

I pulled the walkie-talkie from my pack. I used the code we'd worked out. "Dragonfly, this is Earthworm. Do you read me? Do you read me? Over and out."

No answer.

I tried to contact them two more times — without success. I knew those son-of-a-bitching radios were in A-1 operating condition. That damned le Vieux, sitting in the Peugeot parked up there on the street, must have had his blasted receiver switched off. Unless the thickness of the concrete overhead . . .

Later on I realized that, regardless of the sending set's power, only FM could have done the job right. It would have enabled us to get through the concrete. At any rate, the most serious problem was the inattentiveness of the goddamned Marseillais doing the receiving.

Saturday, May 8, 12:30 A.M.

Now all the equipment lay on the island. The last leg of the journey to the promised land had begun.

Sixty-eight led the way as we moved through the first culvert on all fours, Indian file. I gripped the wire bail of the lantern in my teeth. Other guys looped it around their necks or shoved it under their chins. In addition, we were loaded down like pack mules.

Halfway down that tunnel, a pipe began pouring gallons of foul-smelling filth all over us. Pierre tried to bawl somebody out, but had to shut his mouth fast to keep from being choked by the stream of sewage. Soon, we were covered with stinking filth. In the unsteady beams of our waterproof flashlights we saw that the men ahead of us had puked up their guts. Those poor bastards were moving very slowly; even a few yards of crawling exhausted them. At intervals, we stopped in a swamp of refuse and waited — as the flashlight beams paralyzed bunches of rats that stared at us with their red eyes.

Then, nobody knew how, the column lurched forward again. We crawled, staggering under the weight of our packs, spitting up scum, trembling with cold and horror down there among the bloodworms, maggots, rats, and viruses.

At the end of the tunnel, the sewage was only eighteen inches deep. But we ran into a whole goddamned colony of rats. Some of them scurried away; others swam right alongside us. All of a sudden, one rat decided to cross the culvert just in front of Pierre. Fearing an attack or simply because the beast was repulsive, he flung his bag of tools at it. The enormous rat went right on swimming toward an air shaft without so much as looking around.

"Jesus Christ! I'll never be able to stand those filthy sons of bitches. I'd sooner crawl up to a machine-gun nest with a slingshot than wade two yards through this shit!"

Biki, witnessing the incident, burst out laughing. He appeared to feel right at home, as if he owned the place. That guy was unbelievable.

We started on our way again. Now Pierre clambered over

three drainage pipes where they intersected with the main sewer under the avenue Félix-Faure. He had to cross a culvert one yard wide, bordered by a walkway that was as slippery as ice. Biki went on laughing, so Pierre got sore and wouldn't help him over the obstacle. Biki skidded and went head over heels into the stream. We actually lost sight of him. Then his head appeared three yards downstream. We saw him lunge for his bundle of shorings, which was being carried away by the current. Then the crazy bastard's laughter echoed in the tunnel again.

Not a day went by without one of us taking a spill. Once, la Fouine, sensing that he was about to lose his footing, clutched Rico's arm and pulled him under the water with all our lunches. Another time, I'd teamed up with le Vieux. I had just climbed over the main and was waiting for him. Finally, he came along. Gripping the corner of the wall with both hands, he stretched one leg across the culvert but forgot to let go of the wall. He wound up with his legs on one side of the culvert and his arms on the other. Unable to move, he watched the water swirl past.

"What the hell is going on, for Christ's sake? Hurry, damn it. Get this pack off me, Bert! Hurry!"

He made a desperate effort to regain his balance, but his feet went out from under him and . . . splash! In he went, coming up again about five yards downstream. Snorting, he shook himself while groping blindly for my hand. Even after I got him onto the walkway, he went on coughing and spluttering. Then he looked at me.

"You really get a kick out of that, eh, wise guy?" Then, just as he drew back his fist, pretending to punch me, he slipped. "God damn it!" he yelled. He came up five more yards downstream, floundering, spluttering.

Two months of that. We were going to dig a tunnel twenty-five feet long. Three hundred stinking inches, to be exact. Now we understood why the bank hadn't installed an alarm system on that filthy wall. Two damned months. I knew that for those two months only our sense of humor would keep us from going insane.

1:00 A.M.

Now we were actually inside the Chauvain sewer, the main tunnel of the Nice sewer system. Although we didn't need to crawl, there was so little headroom that we moved with our backs bent double and our knees flexed.

The manual for sewer system inspectors recommends, "Walk stooped, keeping the hands on the thighs." But the superintendent of sewers hadn't written his book with a job like this in mind. Every man was carrying between sixty and one hundred pounds of gear, so we never managed to try the method advocated in the manual. Actually, we stayed underground long enough to tone up the muscles used for work in cramped quarters.

We pushed the equipment ahead, dragged it after us, or just plain carried it. Each man developed a system of his own. You could stand erect by getting down into the channel itself, but then you were in water up to your thighs. We did use this method for going downstream, but it proved exhausting against the current — especially when the stream was deep. Then the current became strong enough to drown a rat.

And we saw thousands of rats down there. In fact, the place grew more rat-infested with each passing day. At first, they would come up to us boldly; soon, however, they found that fear could turn men into enemies. Our flashlights hardly troubled them at the beginning. The rats even seemed to find the lights fascinating — until they learned to associate them with danger.

In any event, the initial reaction of the rats told us exactly what we wanted to know: the sewer workers didn't come down there very often.

Some of us were in mortal terror of rats; others managed to put up with them. A few men didn't seem to mind them in the least. And one actually liked them. I mean Biki. He was a kind of Saint Francis of Assisi when it came to rats. Biki lost his temper only once underground — the night we saw le Tombeur strike a rat with a shovel, then fling it into the watercourse. The creature was too groggy to swim. Biki went plunging into the channel to rescue the drowning rat, which he took in his hands and placed in the safety of an air vent. Despite the punishment it had received, the rat submitted to this handling without even showing its teeth. Bear in mind that cornered rats are very dangerous and their bites can kill within hours.

Biki warned le Tombeur not to hit any more rats with his shovel.

"What are you — crazy or something?" le Tombeur yelled. "You must be out of your fuckin' mind to start protecting rats!"

Biki strode up to le Tombeur, who was built like an ox, and snatched the shovel out of his hands. To our amazement, Biki gave him a punch on the jaw. Stunned, le Tombeur clinched desperately, and both men went rolling into the watercourse.

The fight speedily degenerated into a death struggle. Standing there with our flashlights trained on the two brutes as they beat each other senseless, we were transported back in time thousands of years.

"They're going to kill each other," whispered Pierre, standing at my side in the tunnel.

"You could be right about that."

"What if we separated them?" he asked.

"No, not until they get it out of their systems."

I knew that Biki would never forgive me if I broke up the fight before it took a decisive turn.

Le Tombeur was a head taller than Biki, with powerful shoulders and arms, but he couldn't use his greater size and longer reach in these cramped quarters. Biki was best at infighting. He threw ten punches for every one of le Tombeur's. All at once, Biki belted him right in the family jewels, and he doubled up, choking. Then Biki gave him a couple of vicious rabbit punches. Trapping the big guy's head between his thighs, Biki waded into deeper water, to drown him in the filth.

That was when I tapped Mick on the shoulder. Together, one on each side, we hauled Biki up onto the walkway while Sixty-eight and Rico twisted his ankles to make him let go of le Tombeur's head. The men from Marseille who had been standing behind us rushed forward to get their man out of the water. Pierre looked them both over. The two were in pretty bad shape.

"What were they fighting over, these two clowns?"

"Over a rat."

"Over a rat!" Pierre exclaimed.

He shrugged, as if to say "Okay, if you don't see anything strange about that, neither do I."

1:30 A.M.

We reached the rue Gioffrédo sign that marked a tunnel to the right. We would be moving under the rue Saint-Michel. We had filthy glop in our ears and nostrils. We were covered with muck. But in a few minutes we would be at the foundations of the bank.

We'd done it!

Our bodies slid down those filth-coated walls until our backsides touched the floor. There we sat, exhausted, amazed. On our laps or in the water beside us lay our equipment, but no-body gave a shit anymore.

Barely three hours had elapsed since the job began, and the men were already fed up with the whole damned business. None of them seemed to believe in the job any longer. All you had to do was look at their faces to see it. One by one, the stragglers began to show up. Bringing up the rear came Bouche d'or. He was the only one with a dry cigarette.

"How long will it take us to get through the wall?" asked Bouche d'or.

"A few days . . ." someone began.

"It all depends. If we gave it everything we have . . ."

"Three days, maybe a week," speculated another.

"More than that."

"What the hell do you know about it?"

"I tell you that it won't take that long! I sense it," la Fouine declared.

"Really?"

"Yes, it's kind of a sixth sense."

La Fouine cheered us up with his optimism. I was more objective; I figured about three weeks. Actually, my guess was as far wrong as la Fouine's. One thing was certain: had the men from Marseille suspected that the job would take as long as it did, they would have given up right then and there. I mean, now that they understood the conditions in which they'd be work-ing.

After a few minutes for a smoke, the boys went back for more equipment. They were going to make three more trips apiece — and a few of them would be making a fourth. In the sewers, it was impossible to carry as much gear as you could along the Paillon River.

Mick, Pierre, and I stayed behind — there, near the foundations of the bank. With my jackknife, I scratched a rectangle on the sewer wall measuring thirty-six inches by twenty-nine and located two yards from the manhole at the intersection of the rue Deloye and rue de l'Hôtel-des-Postes. According to my calculations (and God only knows how many nights I'd spent going over them), this was the spot where we should drill. But that didn't stop me from wondering: What if I'm wrong?

At that hour of the night, most people in France should have been sleeping. But not us! Pierre had just hung a camp lantern on each side of my rectangle. Mick had removed a hammer and a cold chisel from his bag. Holding both tools in his hands, he watched, expecting an order. I raised the antenna of my walkie-talkie, then threw a glance at Pierre, who was looking at me in awe. I nodded to Mick, and his hammer came down on the head of the chisel, burying its steel shank in the wall. The job had really started. Personally, at that particular moment, I'd have preferred a breath of fresh air.

With each of Mick's hammer blows, I grew more and more apprehensive. I had to make sure that the clash of steel on steel couldn't be heard in the apartment building that faced the bank.

"Hello, Dragonfly, this is Earthworm. Come in, please. Dragonfly, do you read me? Come in, please. Hello! Hello! One, two, three, four, five, six, seven, eight — do you read me? Come in, Dragonfly, come in. God damn it, Dragonfly, come in! Over . . . Come in, God damn it!"

Suddenly, an infernal squawking filled the tunnel, nearly jarring the radio out of my grasp. I quickly lowered the volume.

"All right, all right! I read you loud and clear. Everything in order."

"Hello, Dragonfly, this is Earthworm. Request a count to adjust reception and tone. Over."

Silence. No answer. That was asking a little too much of le Vieux. I didn't bother asking him again.

Pierre also started in with his hammer and cold chisel, because we had to break through the masonry fast. The "crust" was the noisiest part. Once through it, we could use the pick and the crowbar.

4:00 A.M.

Now the boys who had brought in equipment (there was still more to come) went back out with hemp baskets of rubble to be dumped in the Paillon River. But we kept any good-sized chunks of masonry to use on Monday morning, since we planned to brick up the mouth of our excavation when we knocked off on Monday morning. Obviously, we could work only nights during the week — because of the sewer workers — and then over the weekend from Friday night until Monday morning.

For the moment, our biggest problem was still how to dig a hole big enough to conceal all of our equipment.

Actually, we were inside a large conduit some twenty-nine inches across and forty-eight inches high. Not far from our work site, the conduit was crossed by a fresh-water main six inches in diameter; after that, the conduit widened out under the manhole on the rue de l'Hôtel-des-Postes. That was where I positioned myself, right next to the steel ladder there. I wedged the radio in behind one of the rungs.

While keeping my eyes peeled, I stowed our equipment as best I could. Suddenly, a voice came crackling over the radio. "Hello, Earthworm, do you read me? The coast is clear."

And before I could open my mouth, the voice was gone. Le Vieux must have said his piece and then switched off his walkie-talkie. I couldn't allow things to go on that way. If I needed to transmit a message to him, we were really up shit creek. I decided to go up to the street and settle this business before we had trouble. Furthermore, we needed to keep a better lookout

—just one man watching wasn't enough. Not to mention the fact that this one lookout had to be given a break now and then. And what about all the noise they were making with the sledgehammer? Jesus, I was getting scared.

I handed the walkie-talkie to Bouche d'or and climbed up the ladder to see Pierre and let him know what was on my mind.

"That's taking a chance, you know," he said, looking at me uneasily as I came up in broad daylight.

"I know," I replied, "but we're taking even bigger chances letting things go the way they're going."

"All right. Bring cement when you come back tonight."

"All right."

I lifted a hemp basket full of earth and rubble, then started up the rue Saint-Michel tunnel. At the rue Gioffrédo intersection I caught sight of a flashlight coming in the distance. I waited for the guy and his load so that there wouldn't be any chance of his getting stuck. It was Sixty-eight. He stopped near me and leaned his back against the sludge-coated walls to catch his breath.

"Things seem to be going all right . . . Well, it's a little too soon to tell. Do you know what I was thinking about on my way through the sewer?"

"What were you thinking about?"

"I was thinking about Mireille. Are you going to see her after this is over?"

"Maybe. What do you want me to tell her?"

Heaving himself away from the wall, he gathered his pack.

"Just give her my phone number. I'll give her the message myself. So long!"

And he was off. I hurried under the rue Gioffrédo intersection before one of the other movingmen showed up.

Fifteen minutes later, I was crawling through the last conduit. I glimpsed a light in the distance. Sorry, pal, I'm first, so just back your ass out. All of a sudden, untreated sewage from an overhead pipe came pouring down on me. That didn't matter; I could hear the lapping of the river already, like music to my ears.

I'd finally reached the underground Paillon River. The immense arch of the first tunnel looked like paradise.

Carlos was waiting there for me, with his filthy bandanna and a heavy hydraulic jack. He was the one who'd had to back out. He looked like he was on some kind of pilgrimage, like he was doing penitence for his sins, eyes half-closed and lips vibrating with Spanish litanies. He was about to start out for the next Station of the Cross.

"How's it going, Carlos?"

"Muy bien, gracias."

Biki, seated on our low-lying gravel island, had already tamed a rat, a big fat sucker. Biki was feeding it a heel of bread that he'd swiped from the Marseillais' pack. The beast had him so fascinated that he never heard me coming.

"How long have you been daydreaming?"

He lifted his head slowly.

"Must be ever since the day I met you."

He was caressing the rat, smiling the whole time. His teeth made an astonishing contrast to his mud-streaked face.

"You can't imagine how affectionate these little bastards can be."

"Yes, I can. I practically get nightmares just thinking about it. I'm leaving my basket of dirt here. I'll pick it up tonight."

"Why? You going outside?"

"Yes, I'm going on lookout."

I'd scarcely taken three steps when I froze. God damn it!

Where were the fuckin' keys to the goddamned Volkswagen Kombi?

Oh, Christ, no! I had to go the whole fuckin' way back!

"Hey! Don't go back emptyhanded!"

Jesus Christ! I tied two hydraulic jacks to a length of rope, which I looped around my neck. Then I picked up my flashlight.

On all fours, I dragged the heavy jacks through the deluge of raw sewage, through the stench of rotting turds . . .

The rope was too damned long, so the jacks scraped over the ground. I was scraping everything — my knees, my ass. Reached the Chauvain main sewer. Climbed over culvert, slipped, almost broke my ass. Flashlight carried off by the current. Fog, darkness, shadows. Banged my fuckin' head against everything. Groping, unable to find my way. Couldn't find markers. Hundreds of labyrinthine tunnels; scared shitless of getting lost. Now I stood stock-still, afraid to grope anymore for fear of rat bites. Should I yell or not? Breathe! I had to breathe at any price! I just waited, without moving. I even pissed in my pants; it was wiser. I felt like throwing up. No, I mustn't puke — that would attract rats. The chattering of my teeth drowned out everything else. Should I go back the way I came? No, I had to stay put. I mustn't move. Had to keep breathing. Couldn't breathe too fast. I mustn't give off the smell of fear or the rats would be all over me. Now I really wasn't getting enough oxygen. My air supply *was* cut off! My fuckin' hair stood on end. I was about to scream . . . What was that down there? A faint gleam? No, there was nothing . . . *Yes!* It was a light, a beacon!

"Who's that? You? I thought you . . . Keys? What keys? You cracking up or something?"

"The keys to the Kombi, God damn it!"

"All right, all right, you don't have to get so excited. I'll leave my basket of dirt here and go with you."

"Grab a jack. Go ahead of me, damn it!"

It was la Fouine. We were under the rue Gioffrédo, right in the middle of it. I'd thought that the fork at the rue Saint-Michel was closer. Fortunately, I hadn't gone on groping. I was back at the rue Dache.

Ahead of me, la Fouine wasn't moving forward.

"Why the hell are you going so slow? God damn it, we're in a hurry!"

"It's on account of the jack — I can't get a grip on it. I have to hold it with both hands."

"What about me, god damn it? What do you think I'm doing?"

"You do what you want. Me, I find it easier to go slow."

Easier to go slow . . . If I had any more fuckin' characters like that, I'd give up on the whole job. Well, we were almost there.

They were just standing there, looking at Mick and Pierre instead of doing their work.

"What the fuck are you waiting for? You're just going to stand there watching them dig?"

"We're trying to figure out where to shore up the tunnel. Is that you? I thought that . . . What's going on?"

"What's going on is that I don't have the keys to the damned Kombi."

"Bouche d'or was the one who drove it; he must have them."

"Hey, Bouche d'or! Got the keys for the Kombi?"

"Sure, I still got them."

Sure, he's still got them. What a dunce!

I went up to him.

"Bouche d'or, can you see who it is? It's me, god damn it. Bert."

"What's eating you?"

"I told you to stand by the radio a few minutes ago. Don't you remember?"

"Nobody called! I never moved! Listen, if you just tell me what's eating you, it'll save us both lots of time."

"I told you to stay at the goddamned radio because I was going back up to the street, numskull! Why couldn't you let me know you had the keys to the fuckin' Kombi?"

"What about you, damn it? Couldn't you have asked me for them? You're supposed to be the big brain around here, not me. Anyway, stop the goddamn yelling — I don't go for that! Who the hell do you think you are? My money is at stake in this caper. I'm doing my job just like everybody else."

"What do you want — a raise or something?"

"You give me a pain, acting like a big shot! You understand? A royal pain."

"I had to crawl through the sewers three times on account of you, jerk! What am I supposed to do — wait all day before I go outside?"

"Bert Spaggiari, maybe no one ever told you, but I'm . . ."

"They told me! They told me all about you! Now hand over those keys!"

"Here's your damned keys. But from now on watch how you talk to me, Bert. You're just a crummy photographer who lost the goddamned war and you still haven't gotten over it. Do anything you want, but just stay off my back! If you don't, you'll wish you did."

"We'll see about that."

I turned and left.

Just between you and me, Bouche d'or wasn't exactly meek.

He had a reputation as a street fighter. He was all keyed up and so was I. We were all on edge. That's why I didn't press the issue.

Twenty minutes later, I was standing on the banks of the underground Paillon River, in the vast tunnel. It must have been 5:30 A.M. Biki was squatting with his pants down, a hundred yards away. I started to wash my hands and face in the icy water of the stream, but the draft coming in off the Mediterranean was so cold that I gave up.

Half a mile farther on, I reached the manhole outside the Café L'Aube de l'Islam, where we'd entered the sewer. I'd hidden a change of clothing in a dark corner there. The others had carried their things up to the island in the river. I lit a camp lantern. I stripped and sat down in the clear water of the Paillon.

Clear but icy. It was waist-deep. I needed to lie down in the water and finally did. It was so freezing that my heart nearly stopped. Jesus Christ, I felt like I was going to die of shock. I scrambled to my feet and started running in place to get the circulation back.

After that, I rubbed myself all over with eau de cologne and pulled on fresh underwear.

Despite this, I stank of sewage. People were going to cross the fuckin' street just to avoid me.

I knew that it must be light outside. But it was out of the question to raise the manhole cover. Besides, I couldn't have managed it alone. The only way out was to follow the river upstream until it came out in the open. In other words, I'd have to walk upstream as far as the Palais des Expositions, about half a mile away.

I did that stretch of dry riverbed in a few minutes. At that time of day there were no kids or *pétanque* bowlers around. I came out through the third arch. That was the easiest place. I stood facing a concrete pillar, pretending to urinate, craning my neck to make sure that there was no one on the promenade back of the Palais des Expositions. Then I scrambled up the rocky bank on the left. I loosened the cuffs of my trousers, which had been tucked into my boot tops. I thrust my hands into my pockets and began whistling like a guy who's out walking his dog. I headed for the grassy bank that borders the avenue du Maréchal-Lyautey.

A flatfoot walked by. Aside from him, not a soul around. I swung my leg over the railing, and there I was, back on the sidewalks of Nice. Like Monsieur Jean Average in person.

Not an open café in sight. Just as well; I stank to high heaven. All the same, maybe some nice little neighborhood café on a side street . . .

Six A.M. Maybe six-fifteen. I wasn't sure; my watch had stopped. A few cars, some motorbikes. I walked drunkenly. Being out in the open was dizzying. You have to do time in solitary to understand how I felt. All those streets that I knew by heart. I let the wind blow through my brain, the chill wind of daybreak. I crossed the esplanade and headed for the avenue Gallieni. I'd spent the last few years in a closet. Foolishly, I'd had the idea that all my problems would be solved with the passing of time. Time doesn't solve anything. It just makes you more demanding, that's all. You can struggle as much as you want — it's no use. You're fucked. After you hit forty, you go downhill. Just when you ought to be happy, you're down in the dumps. When you're miserable, you imagine you're happy. I must have fought too many battles for nothing. I still have a lot going for me. If I could just play my cards right, maybe I could get started again.

After passing the Jean-Bouin Stadium, I went by a garbage

Albert Spaggiari's photo store on the Route de Marseille in Nice. *Photo Albin Michel*

The mouth of the Paillon River under the Promenade des Anglais. The river cuts across another forty yards of beach before emptying into the Mediterranean. *Photo Albin Michel*

L'Aube de l'Islam, the Arab café located near the manhole that the robbers used for the first few weeks. *Photo Albin Michel*

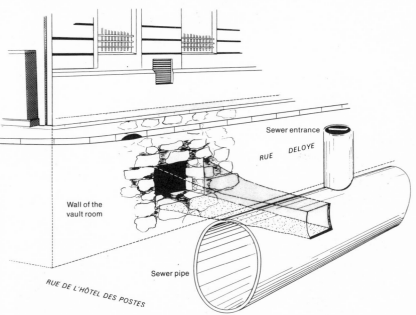

The Société Générale bank at the corner of the rue Hôtel-des-Postes and the rue Deloye. The manhole used by the robbers practically touches the pedestrian crosswalk. At the far end of the building are the night watchman's quarters. *Photo Albin Michel*

The mouth of the conduit where Nice's Paillon River cuts underground. Above, the back of the Palais des Expositions. In the foreground, a railway bridge. *Photo Albin Michel*

The banks of the Paillon River between the Vincent-Auriol Bridge and the second railway bridge (on the right). In the center of this photo appears the service road Spaggiari used to bring the Land Rover down onto the riverbed. *Photo Albin Michel*

The news is out. Box-holders wait vainly outside the Société Générale. *Photo
Gilbert Castiès*

Manhole on the rue Deloye through which Spaggiari made his first reconnaissance. *Photo Gilbert Castiès*

The inspectors bring out the first tanks. *Photo Gilbert Castiès*

Hose used for ventilating tunnel. *Photo Gilbert Castiès*

Some of the tanks were never used. *Photo Gilbert Castiès*

The Félix-Faure main sewer where it comes out at the place Masséna garage. *Photo Gilbert Castiès*

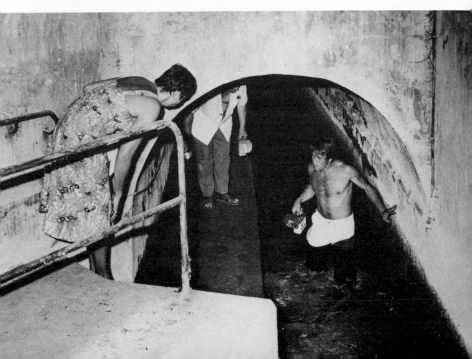

The robbers tapped a source of electric power—the fluorescent light in an underground garage. *Photo Gilbert Castiès*

The inspectors reeling in part of the four hundred yards of electric wire that went from the tunnel to the place Masséna garage. *Photo Gilbert Castiès*

Albert Spaggiari emerges from police headquarters after forty-eight consecutive hours of questioning. *Photo Gilbert Castiès*

Albert Spaggiari on his way to the Nice branch of the Société Générale for a reconstruction of the crime. *Photo Gilbert Castiès*

The Wild Geese. Albert Spaggiari spent several years restoring this old chalet in the Alps. *Photo Gilbert Castiès*

Thursday, March 10, 1977. At about 5:00 P.M., Albert Spaggiari climbs out onto the ledge of a third-story window in the courthouse — and escapes. *Photo Gilbert Castiès*

The dent in the roof of the Renault that Albert Spaggiari used to cushion the impact of his jump. *Photo Gilbert Castiès*

Albert Spaggiari and his lawyer, Maître Jacques Peyrat, coming out of the examining judge's chamber. *Photo Gilbert Castiès*

truck and a busload of cops. On the other side of the boulevard, the racket of a motorcycle was waking up the whole neighborhood. Yes, with time you become more demanding. Or else you make believe; you pretend that everything is just fine. This wouldn't be the first time that everything was "just fine." I'd been through all that before. Tomorrow, I'd buy myself the Fiji Islands; I'd build my own mountains. It didn't matter that I stank of untreated sewage.

When I'd been a political prisoner, I'd met some men who really meant something to me. I also met some of the worst people in my life. Empty minds, without a spark of originality, without the slightest passion. Wretched, beaten souls who had forged their own chains. It was a golden captivity, where all I had to do was wait for it to be over. Yet I've known dozens of vile prisons that were country clubs compared to that one. It was in that hell of religious and bourgeois stupidity that I had the same dream over and over. I was back on the farm where I'd grown up. In the village of Sainte-Marguerite, near Gap. I was swimming blissfully in the manure pit. I liked that dream. It made me feel purified. Whenever I had that dream, I was back in the sunshine, close to the earth, living a simple animal existence. I was back with my mother. But I had to admit that when the dream came true, when I actually did wade through night soil, it wasn't quite the same feeling.

I got in behind the wheel of the Volkswagen Kombi and drove along the quai Saint-Jean, paralleling the sea. The bistros were starting to open. There I was on the place Masséna. I headed up the rue Gioffrédo. One more left, and then, a few seconds later, I pulled over to the curb and got out.

I walked across the deserted intersection, stopping in the middle. A couple of yards under me, I told myself, the guys are digging. I had the vague impression that I could feel the vibration from the jackhammer in the balls of my feet. It was just my imagination. I started strolling along the sidewalks. Up and down. It couldn't be my imagination. I also had the feeling that I could hear hammer blows. Jesus Christ, it was like being drunk. I couldn't trust my own judgment. The Peugeot was parked at the corner in front of the café.

I went there. Le Vieux wasn't inside. He must have gone for a walk around the block. Or he was in some bar having a drink. Naturally, he'd locked all the damned doors. While waiting, I strolled along the sidewalk outside the bank and stopped two yards from the manhole, exactly over the spot where they were tunneling our gallery. I took out a cigar. I lit it. I'd even forgotten to smoke since coming up out of the sewers. That says something about the state I . . . God damn it! I wasn't crazy! *I did hear noise!* No doubt about it, I could hear a kind of sputtering or crackling. Just then I also heard footsteps approaching. They were coming from the rue de l'Hôtel-des-Postes. In four or five seconds the guy would pass me. I started to cough as hard as I could, trying to muffle the hammering down below.

It was le Vieux.

He glared at me as if he'd caught me stealing something.

"What the hell are you doing here?"

"What about you? What are you doing, for Christ's sake?"

"I'm making my goddamned rounds," he said. I don't know why, but I burst out laughing. I just couldn't hold it in. The more I looked at his face, the harder I laughed. Besides, I remembered how he'd split his sides laughing at that very spot only a few weeks before. I was struck by the coincidence, and that made my laughter subside. He just shrugged and turned away. He was headed for the truck. I caught up with him.

"Say, I hear some kind of crackling noise. Don't you hear it?"

"That's the switchboxes on the corner. They control the traffic lights."

I walked over to check. Sure enough, that's what it was. What a relief! I led le Vieux to the truck.

"What did I ever do to rate a fuckin' guy like you, Castapiagne?"

He unlocked the door of the truck and climbed in.

"You going to stay here very long?" he asked.

"Why?"

"You stink to high heaven, that's why."

I picked up the walkie-talkie that was plugged into the vehicle's outside aerial.

"I really stink?"

"It smells like you crapped in your pants."

"Hello, this is Dragonfly calling Earthworm. Do you read me? Come in, please."

"Read you loud and clear, Dragonfly. Over." It was the voice of Bouche d'or.

"Ten seconds after you hear my last word, ask them to make as much racket as they can. Over."

"Will do. Over."

"Over and out."

I handed the walkie-talkie to le Vieux and jogged back to the manhole. I heard some vague, faraway sounds. Actually, they were almost inaudible. Once the traffic noise started, the people in the neighborhood wouldn't hear a thing. Besides, the guys in the tunnel were deliberately trying to make a racket.

I walked back to the truck to call Bouche d'or. I told him that everything was okay at this stage.

Next, I gave le Vieux specific orders about the radio and about his work as a lookout. He kept nodding his head as he listened. He was smoking one cigarette after another and had all the windows lowered.

"You think it would be too risky if I went in someplace for a cup of coffee?"

"Go ahead," he replied. "Personally, I can't stand the way you stink."

He reached over the back of the seat and brought up a raincoat.

"Here, put this on and button it up good before you go into a café. If you ever open the damned thing, you'll kill everybody at the bar."

A few seconds later, I was entering the Café Olympia, at the corner of the rue Pastorelli and the rue Deloye. I ordered a double espresso through clenched teeth so that the proprietor wouldn't get a whiff of my sewer breath. After that, I phoned Mireille and asked her to have the bath ready.

"And dump a whole box of bubble bath in it."

"What are you — crazy? That'll take your skin off," she said.

"I don't care. A whole damned box of the stuff."

It became our favorite term. For the shift coming out of the tunnel, bubble bath meant rest, bliss, coffee . . .

Bubble bath, we loved the fuckin' stuff.

The bath was ready when I got home. Blue, hot, sudsy. I slid in blissfully, ecstatically, euphorically. Half an hour later, Mireille came in to scrub my back. Next, I rinsed myself under the shower in the other bathroom.

Oh, the luxury of it all!

Afterward, I rubbed myself all over with eau de cologne, pulled on a silk robe, and went downstairs to eat the steak and eggs that Mireille had fixed for me.

Then came the nap. A long, long nap. So long that a few hours seemed like ten centuries. I opened my eyes when a woman's hair brushed across my back, and a tongue made grazing contact with my neck, with my ear. I rolled over and put my arms around Mireille.

O Mireille, goddess of whores! O Mireille, mother, wife, and light of my life, how good you were to us.

You never demanded anything; you never refused us anything. You were attentive to our every desire, to our slightest need, to our tiniest scratch or cut. Without your warmth, some of us would have given up, and then the job would have become much harder.

I knew each morning you'd be there to open the door, that my bath would be ready, that you would be ready.

O Mireille bubble bath!

CHAPTER 15

A Brilliant Idea

"YOU'RE THE FIRST MAN I've ever met who didn't smoke a cigarette afterward."

"That must mean I'm a hell of a lot better than all the rest. Where's my underpants and my socks? I had them somewhere . . ."

"On the chair."

"Bravo! Clean underwear, a fresh shirt, suit pressed. You're like some kind of fairy godmother."

"Bert, do you think I'm good-looking? I mean, really good-looking?"

"You're a real knockout, and you know it perfectly well."

"I need to be told I'm beautiful. It's important to me. That's all I have."

"Come on, now. Why should a nice girl like you talk that kind of nonsense? I think you're just fishing for . . ."

Mireille got to her feet and walked over to the big mirror. She gazed at her nude body with an almost total lack of shame.

"Do you know which one of you I like best?"

"Keep it to yourself. Up till now everything's been going fine. Don't start trouble."

"I want to tell you because you're the leader."

"The leader doesn't want to know."

"You're in a bad mood all of a sudden."

"Get dressed, will you?"

"That's the nicest thing you've ever said to me, Bert. What do you say? It's only two o'clock. Do you want . . . ?"

"I want you to get dressed. Take my car and go buy a bag of cement. Just leave it at the place I'm going to mark for you on a piece of paper."

"A bag of cement! Boy, when you start getting romantic, there's no way to stop you. What the hell am I supposed to wear to buy the cement? I mean, when they sling the bag over my shoulder, maybe I shouldn't be in a fur coat. All right, I know I'm annoying you . . . But there's one thing I wanted to ask you, just out of curiosity. Do you carry a gun when you go out?"

"Yes."

I pulled on my jacket. I took a 500-franc note from my pocket and handed it to her.

"This is my favorite weapon. You just aim this at the guy and he'll give you the cement. So long, sweetheart."

It was 2:15 P.M. I climbed into the VW Kombi and drove off to see le Vieux.

Ten minutes later, I was down on one knee, tying my shoe, next to the manhole on the rue Deloye. Not a sound came through. Just as I straightened up, a girl said, "Hello, Monsieur Spaggiari."

"Oh . . . er . . . hello," I managed to mumble, almost swallowing my cigar in the process. Oh, Christ, what rotten luck! The girl continued on her way. At least, my first impulse had been right: instead of running away, I'd remained standing there beside some racks for parking bicycles. Every so often I glanced at my watch, like somebody who had a date. Now I had the feeling that every passerby was snapping my picture; that the sales girls were watching me from behind the curtains of shoe-store windows; that they were going to remember me for the composite picture. What about the fish market? That was even worse; they pretended not to see me. And the waiters from the restaurant, L'Orchidée Bleue, what about them? Orientals were supposed to have incredible memories for faces. And all the while, a heavyset man walked up and down the sidewalk across the way. A cop for sure!

I was seeing cops everywhere. Still worse, I saw people I knew, customers, even an old pal on a motorbike, who went right by without seeing me. I was headed for a goddamned heart condition. I looked at my watch one last time and then made for the shelter of the Peugeot.

"Quit worrying," le Vieux told me. "Nobody's seen you in the street. You're like a ghost. Once I was coming out of a bank I'd just stuck up and who do I pass but my own cousin. He didn't even recognize me!"

Another time, he said, while serving his apprenticeship in Paris, he'd spent three days in front of a bank waiting for a courier who decided not to show. He'd been standing right near a taxi stand, a bus stop, and, across the way, a little cigar store. And not one of those people had been able to describe him.

But it wasn't that way for me. Not just then. I couldn't walk down the block without bumping into an old acquaintance.

Around 6:00 P.M. I called the boys. Everything was going smoothly. They were working with the jackhammer in a mixture of stone and clay. They didn't need me, so I stayed with le Vieux on lookout. I'd go back down to the boys the following night with the bag of cement.

I remember thinking just then that it might take us more than three weeks to reach the vault. And while I stood gazing at the bank, just across the street, it seemed impossible not to reach it. It also seemed impossible to get there without problems.

In all my wars, big and small, I'd never worked with anything but idiots, guys so dumb that they managed to foul up right away. This time, my main concern had been recruiting a regular commando unit. I'd been lucky enough to get two refusals right away, and that's why everything went smoothly.

Three months before, I'd attempted to raise the funds necessary for running the caper all by myself. I'd bumped into one friend who still owed me a certain sum on a job that I'd done for him several months before.

"Put the money you owe me into this caper."

"I still haven't gotten my payoff, I swear. I'm flat broke."

I knew he was lying, but what could I do?

Then I went to see another contact. A solid guy who only gave you straight answers. But he was in a financial bind. Woman trouble and waning health.

"And then there's this wild plan of yours. Personally, I think it's a lot of bunk. You do too much daydreaming," he told me.

That may give you some idea of what I was up against.

Yes, I was lucky, all right. Those two fellows would have turned my "heist of the century" into small potatoes.

Le Vieux was asleep, stretched out in the back of the huge truck, next to the leftovers of a sandwich and a half-empty bottle of red wine. Night had fallen on the city.

A night like any other night. Wearing more makeup than in the daytime, the streetwalkers mingled with the first drunks of the evening. The porno movie houses on the avenue Jean-Médecin emptied and filled with the regularity of the tides. Whores would get together in groups of three or four, then scatter. A transvestite leaned his back against the truck. His act consisted of walking toward the avenue to attract some timid soul. Then he'd swing his hips on the way back. About 1:00 A.M., a man stopped near the Peugeot; he caught sight of me and went hurrying away like a guilty thing. At 2:30 A.M., a sanitation worker uncapped a hydrant and started hosing down the street, moving toward the bank as he went.

"Come in, Earthworm."

"This is Earthworm."

"Avoid any noise; they're cleaning the street up here. Over and out."

Next, I woke up le Vieux. Then I stretched out in the back of the truck and slept until morning.

Sunday, May 9, 8:00 A.M.

It was my turn to go and have a cup of coffee. I got out of the truck, stretching. A fine day was starting. Bam! I ran smack into a fellow named Mimile, the bank guard. Twenty minutes later, on the way back from breakfast, bang! I bumped into Mimile again. This time he looked me up and down.

Oh, Christ!

Quickly, I thought up an alibi in case he . . . I'd lost my lighter. It was a gift from my wife. He really did give me a funny look — as if I wasn't the type who'd own a lighter.

I waited until he disappeared and went back to my hiding place in the back of the truck.

That's where I spent my Sunday, alongside le Vieux, who never stopped his damned snoring. My legs even fell asleep. Then I saw Mimile emerge from his glassed-in booth.

I left the truck a quarter of an hour later and headed for the Café L'Aube de l'Islam. I parked the Kombi in the exact spot where I'd found it the morning before.

It was 5:00 P.M. when I made my way to the Palais des Expositions. I walked around the building till I reached the Paillon River.

On a Sunday afternoon, the Paillon becomes a recreation area. Some stretches of the riverbed have been leveled, and people play volley ball there. And sometimes you'll see a group of bowlers playing *pétanque*. On the far bank, a cluster of people might be training an Irish setter. Kids use the dry river-bed to test their cross-country motorcycles; others fly remote-controlled model planes under the arches of the Paillon.

I'd had an idea a little earlier in the afternoon. An idea for carrying the tanks of acetylene. We were going to need lots of them. These steel cylinders are extremely heavy and cumbersome. It wasn't going to be any cinch getting them down the manhole. We were going to need a winch — and lots of time. In other words, we just couldn't get the tanks down unnoticed. The whole business of the acetylene was risky.

It occurred to me that the perfect solution was to load the acetylene tanks into a stolen Land Rover and drive the stuff right up the underground Paillon as far as the sewers. The river's tunnels were so cavernous, you could drive a goddamned truck through them. A Land Rover would do fine, because it's designed for rough terrain and has a four-wheel drive. It's even capable of fording shallow rivers.

I simply had to make sure that we'd have access to the riverbed. That's what I'd come to check.

I was strolling among the people playing volley ball and *pétanque,* twisting my ankles on the rounded stones, when all of a sudden . . . "Monsieur Spaggiari! What are you doing around here?"

I didn't recognize the man's face at all; his accent wasn't from Nice, but Paris.

"I might ask you the same question," I retorted, scrutinizing his face. I'd never seen the guy before in my life. How the fuck did he know my goddamned name?

He just stood there in front of me with the sly look of somebody putting you through a game of twenty questions.

"You can't place my face?" he asked, finally.

"No."

"I'm a policeman. I live just over there . . ." He stretched out an arm in one direction. He wasn't lying. There was a fuckin' police station two hundred yards farther up the banks of the Paillon River. "So you don't recognize me, eh? Well, I never forget a face. But after all, that's my job. What are you doing around here?

"I'm looking for a male Doberman to mate with my younger bitch. They told me that . . . But it turned out that the dog wasn't a pure Doberman. Well, I've got to be going."

"So long. See you again."

See you again! Jesus Christ! I was weak in the knees as I climbed back up the grassy bank. I spotted my car at the place I'd asked Mireille to leave it. The bag of cement was in the trunk. From that angle, everything was going smoothly. I got behind the wheel and drove off. I'd go back to my research later. That cop on his day off — he'd scared the shit out of me.

I drove around the Société Générale branch a couple of times, slowly, like somebody riding aimlessly. As I went by, le Vieux nodded to me. According to him, everything was fine.

Then I went to a restaurant and waited for darkness to fall.

8:00 P.M.

I parked my car just behind the railroad bridge. Twenty yards away was the Café Carré d'As, where Mireille had left the car. The customers at that bar are mostly policemen from the nearby headquarters, and guards from the prison.

Across the way, leaning or sitting on the railing along the Paillon, crowds of teen-agers were engaged in conversation or necking. On the promenade behind the Palais des Expositions, a few queers were trying to make a pickup, and some old biddies walked their dogs. The kind of women that stop gossiping when you come near. They stare at you as if you were planning a crime, and then they whisper, turning to watch you go by, "One of those fresh punks!"

On the other side, an Arab rag-picker was unloading a little wagon and lugging his booty under the first archway of the Paillon River. He lived there, but he wouldn't bother us. He got up in the middle of the night and left to go out scavenging. Nor would the kids get in our way when we went in through there rather than the manhole at the Café L'Aube de l'Islam. Quite the contrary, for they became so accustomed to seeing us every night, they would always say hello. And later on, when the papers plastered "the heist of the century" on the front page and when the bank offered a "colossal reward" of one million francs for anyone giving information leading to the arrest of the robbers, not one of those kids went to the cops.

Only one of the old biddies with the dogs went around tattling. You stupid old slut, did you really believe they'd hand you a million francs for your goddamned gossip?

I went on coming and going under the critical eyes of the old women, who never stopped yapping. It was impossible for me to get under the archways without being spotted.

I had to wait until midnight to unload the bag of cement (over which I'd carefully pulled a watertight plastic wrapper) from the trunk of my car and go down the banks of the Paillon. Now I had to make my way through a mile-long stretch of dark tunnel, staggering over the uneven ground with a hundred pounds on my shoulder. An icy draft blew through the subterranean gallery, evaporating the sweat that bathed my body, chilling me to the bone. It was always cold like that, yet none of us ever got sick.

Three quarters of an hour later, I dropped my burden on the gravel island. Mike and Pierre were asleep there, lying on boards.

I went straight into the sewers without wasting time. I kissed my nice clean scent good-by. The bag of cement now seemed to weigh two hundred pounds. Farther on, I met up with the first guys on the bucket brigade. Two by two, they were dumping tons of earth into the Gioffrédo main sewer. They were right; it was closer, and the swift current soon carried the dirt away.

Half an hour later, I joined the bucket brigade. Teaming up with Hervé, I worked until two or three in the morning. That night, adventure consisted of a hemp basket containing sixty pounds of dirt. The stuff had to be moved over a distance of more than one hundred yards through a conduit five feet high. Except this tunnel was full of rusty pipes and outlets that kept spewing streams of raw sewage. Furthermore, this oval tunnel was rounded at the bottom. Footing became treacherous. Our heads and shoulders collided constantly with the concrete walls. In no time, we were coated with filth.

I thought about my mother's advice: "Always brush your teeth carefully, dear. And whatever you do, don't catch a cold. Make sure you carry a . . ."

Every now and then, we took a little break when the tempo of the tunnel-digging slowed down. All of a sudden, le Tombeur, who was sitting in a bypass, let out a shriek. A rat was foraging in his pocket. He flung it at la Fouine, squatting next to him. The son of a bitch jumped like he'd received an electric shock, and cracked his skull against a pipe. Man overboard.

Monday, May 10, 3:30 A.M.

The gallery was now five feet deep and solidly shored up. There we stored the most important equipment. The rest — lumber, pails, etc. — was concealed in other places, where it wouldn't attract attention.

Mick and Gigi hastily built a wall, using the cement and big rocks they'd stored. Afterward, they plastered the new masonry with mud. The camouflage was perfect.

"Earthworm to Dragonfly. Assemble at five, according to plan. Do you read me? Come in, please."

"Yeah."

Our weariness disappeared like magic. The boys began cracking jokes as they hurried back to the underground river, back to the open air, a bubble bath, and a real dinner.

In the river tunnel, Bouche d'or dropped his arm around my shoulders. "Come on, we'll make it all right. Don't let things get you down."

The team from Marseille climbed into the Volkswagen Kombi, and we boarded the Peugeot. It wasn't going to be long before sunrise.

"Hey, there!" Pierre waved his arm at us from the Volkswagen. "Briefing tonight at eight o'clock in the villa! *Ciao!*"

Only le Vieux and I had heard him. In the back of the truck, the others were drawing straws to see who'd have first crack at the shower and the bathtub. They also drew straws to see who'd have first crack at Mireille. Every three hours after that, another guy would get his turn.

CHAPTER 16

A Fake Beard and a Pair of Glasses

Same day, the villa, 8:10 P.M.

While the old mansion turned red in the setting sun and the wildflowers in the orchard began to close, you could hear: "Ow, my aching back! Oh, Jesus, my feet are numb! Look at my hands! Feel this goddamned bump on my skull! How's this for a fuckin' black-and-blue mark?"

"Eat a lot to get your strength back," somebody said.

Pierre and Mathieu stuffed themselves. They got their strength back, all right.

"And what about me? You think I had it so easy?" le Vieux complained, having spent a whole damned weekend in the truck.

Bouche d'or was swinging in a hammock outside, with a mug of black coffee beside him. I gave him a cigar.

As I held the match for him, I remembered noticing the bristles on his Adam's apple, like somebody who uses an electric razor. His face was deeply lined, but a boyish gleam still lurked in his eyes.

"What are you going to do with your share?" he asked, as if the same question was troubling him.

I sat down at the base of the palm tree, tossing a few pebbles up and down in my hand. "I'll certainly keep some of it and donate the rest to a good cause."

"You guys make me laugh with your political parties. What the hell, everybody knows that those son-of-a-bitching politicians are all rotten. And you idealists are even worse!"

"You think it's better to bury your head in the sand?"

"Absolutely. If everyone paid attention to his own business, the world would be a better place. I've been around. I see through that fucked-up smile of yours. You go around looking as though you couldn't care less, but I know that something's gnawing at you inside. What is it?"

"For the time being, it's the bank. Afterward, everything will go all right. I'm sure of it."

"Nobody's *that* lucky, Bert."

"Who knows? Everyone's luck changes sometime."

"Well, just don't saw the branch you're sitting on. Quit chasing after daydreams. One of these days you'll wind up alone, with your back to the wall, and you know what . . ."

That was when I got up and went behind the garage to take a piss. My urine was clear as water. That reminded me of a doctor I'd known when I was a boy. He used to say "Silver piss is better than golden piss." The son of a bitch would have been pleased with mine, all right.

"Bert! Hey, Bert! Where's Bert! Berrrrt!"

I pulled the chain to flush the toilet.

"Yeah, I'm coming."

The briefing started. No apéritif, no whiskey; just coffee. Everybody was in the living room. The two crews were mixed together. The boys had begun to suffer together. The observation period was over; now it was all one gang. For better or for worse. And, as it turned out, we got both.

Pierre sat on the couch between Mick and la Fouine. He opened the session. That was the first time I'd ever seen him call a meeting to order from a sitting position. He wasn't trying to make his authority felt anymore.

"First point: the organization of work. I think that there should only be five of us down in the tunnel during the week. That would mean three from your bunch, two from mine. What do you think, Bert?"

"I agree. The hole is too small. Overcrowding won't get us anywhere. Besides, if we reduce the size of the crew, we minimize the risk. Gigi and Biki will come down with me tonight."

Pierre turned and picked his crew. "Le Vieux, Le Tombeur."

The two men nodded. I took the floor again.

"As for *how* we go underground, I think we should stick to the manhole in front of the Café l'Aube de l'Islam. For the time being, at least. On the other hand, it would be best to use the Paillon River exit for coming back up."

"Why not go *down* that way, as well?"

"It might be possible. There's just one problem with that: too many people around at night. Another thing: we've got to set up a system of rotation for the lookouts. There have to be two of them at all times. I suggest that each pair of lookouts stay on for twenty-four-hour shifts.

"All right. For the first shift, I'm assigning la Fouine and Hervé. Hervé, you'll also drive the crew to L'Aube de l'Islam tonight and pick them up tomorrow. Now, about the signals; we haven't been running things too fuckin' well."

"That's right. You know, what really bothers me is that one of our conversations could be intercepted. It's fairly unlikely, but it could happen."

"What can we do about it?"

"I thought up a code that would be less dangerous. But let's go over the other points right now; I'll explain the code later."

Pierre looked around the room. "Any other suggestions?"

Mick got to his feet and put his coffee mug on the table. "We're going to need a new set of drill bits every day."

"We'll also have to change the miner's bars fairly often," said Sixty-eight.

"Something will be done about that," Pierre replied, nodding at Bouche d'or.

The clock in the next room chimed nine.

Now we took up the question of the excavated dirt. I recommended the Indo-Chinese method, involving two straw baskets — smaller than the hemp ones we had — suspended from a yoke. Excavation would go faster that way and be less tiring.

The same night, about eleven, shortly after the Café l'Aube de l'Islam closed its doors, Biki, Gigi, le Vieux, le Tombeur, and I climbed down into the main sewer leading into the underground Paillon.

For le Vieux, this was the baptism of filth. "Oh, Christ! It's dark in here! Isn't there any damned electricity in this son-of-a-bitching place? Oh, shit! Not so fast. I'm twisting my goddamned ankles. Not so fast, god damn it! Oh, shit, that does it! I've sprained my fuckin' ankle. God damn it! I can't walk! I've had it. Jesus Christ, my ankle is all fucked up. Phone Hervé and tell him to come and get me. Christ, that hurts something awful . . . Oh, Jesus!"

"Come on, Castapiagne, keep going!"

"Look, I'd rather pull an armed robbery than all this nonsense. And what's that goddamned draft? Where's that wind coming from? I'm going to catch my death of cold. I don't know about money, but I know I'm going to get pneumonia. I can feel the dampness in my sinuses. Laugh all you want, wise guy! I had tuberculosis. Go ahead, you think it's so funny . . . If I'd only known . . ."

"You would have brought your nose drops."

And we were only under the vaulted ceilings of the Paillon. You should have heard him a while later, when he had to get down on all fours in the filth to enter the sewers.

"Quit pushing! No shit, boys; I've had it. I fuckin' well give up."

"Thirty to forty million francs, le Vieux."

"I don't give a damn. I don't give a goddamn about your money. You can fuckin' well keep it."

"You must love my body if you're letting me have your share of the loot."

"Ah, shut up! I don't want to talk about it anymore. My fuckin' mind is made up. I know it's a serious decision . . . Quit the goddamned pushing, will you? Jesus Christ! What the fuck am I touching? Oh, God! Rats! *Rats!* Son of a bitch, I don't have my rod . . . Oh, Jesus, watch out . . . I'm going under . . . God damn it! I'm drowning. Son of a bitch, don't touch me! Leave me the fuck alone! I refuse to move — do you understand? I swear that I'm through with the whole fuckin' job!"

With Biki, it was just the opposite. He enjoyed being down there and volunteered to work every night.

Finally, we reached the work site and began to tear down the wall that concealed the tunnel mouth. Next, we removed the equipment and organized ourselves for the actual work of digging. Since le Vieux didn't want to wander through the sewers, we put him to work digging. Besides, he was short — that was an advantage. The gallery measured three feet high by two and a half feet wide. Le Vieux teamed up with Gigi.

Now we weren't tunneling through earth but through rocks. There were only three of us to cart away the excavated material, so we never stopped moving back and forth through the filth with our hemp baskets. We worked at top speed, for the job could only be done at night during the week. That gave us just a few hours.

While he dug the gallery, Gigi wore a helmet wired for radio reception. Actually, it was tuned in to the walkie-talkie. Our system of communication had been simplified to the extreme. When the lookout tapped his fingernail against the microphone it meant, "Stop digging; silence." When he breathed into the micro twice, it meant that the danger had passed and that work could resume normally. Continued fingernail tapping was serious. That meant, "Stop everything until further orders."

Biki and Gigi wedged the last shorings into place. Then the equipment was put away and the wall rebuilt. We left the tunnel at 5:00 A.M., exiting behind the Palais des Expositions.

It was broad daylight.

We'd miscalculated.

I ventured out first. I started to climb the embankment but remembered the policeman who'd accosted me the day before. Oh, Christ! It doesn't take much to wreck everything. Not a person in sight. Hervé had parked the VW Kombi on the grassy shoulder of the avenue du Maréchal-Lyautey, near the railing. I beckoned to the others behind me. They moved into the open.

We couldn't expect to pull off a stunt like that every morning, not without getting ourselves nabbed. That's what I was thinking as I took my bath.

Besides, that day I was really on edge. The boys knew it and left me alone. I just had a snack and went straight to bed. It was my turn with Mireille. Even that wasn't enough to calm my jangled nerves.

I dragged myself out of bed at noon. I borrowed a jacket (at least two sizes too big) from Mick and instructed Sixty-eight to let Pierre know that I'd be in front of the Café L'Aube de l'Islam at 11:00 P.M. and that I had to talk to him.

At 1:00 P.M., I slid behind the wheel of the car. I needed a fake beard and a pair of glasses. And a golf cap, as well. I didn't have any problem finding the cap, but it was 4:00 P.M. before I got the rest of the stuff.

As soon as I had my disguise, I made straight for the Paillon. That's where I had to go, and I didn't want to run the risk of being spotted. I parked my car on the boulevard Jean-Baptiste-Vérani, then walked across the footbridge. I was even harder to recognize because I'd put on three sweaters under Mick's jacket. They gave me the appearance of being much heavier.

I passed the Café Carré d'As and strolled along the balustrade that borders the Paillon River. I went past the police barracks. After that, there's a police station. (The place is crawling with cops.) Wearing an innocent look, I observed both banks of the river. About six hundred yards from there, after the second railway bridge, I spotted a kind of dirt parking lot on the river bank. Some guy had even driven right down to the water's edge to wash his car.

I'd found my road. Located on the other side of the river, just opposite the highway department warehouse, it was simply a strip of beaten earth that sloped down gradually to a kind of level place used as a parking lot. Farther down, after a few uneven stretches, a sloping service road took you down to the dry bed of the Paillon. You could even drive a panel truck through there.

But there was still one problem with the place where the Paillon went underground: two rails barred the entrance to the river just under the archways. The rails must have been put there to keep kids out. One pair of rails per arch, secured to the concrete by means of four bolts. If my memory served, some of the bolts were missing. Apparently, the highway department sometimes forgot to replace them after working under the archways. At any rate, they would remove the rails whenever the river was swollen.

Theoretically, that wasn't a real problem. No, not theoretically. But when you got down to cases, it was. Everything became a problem when you got down to cases.

I retraced my steps back to my car. I could have gone the long way over the Vincent-Auriol Bridge and taken the other boulevard. No, I went back along the same route.

Just after the orphanage, a flock of kids lined the balustrade along the Paillon, watching a game of volley ball in progress below.

Over the running commentary, I heard one boy say, "My brother's doing pretty good since he set himself up on the Route de Marseille. He told me he might be able to take me in with him."

"I saw him the other day; he was in the Sportifs with some broad . . ."

I kept right on going. The Bar des Sportifs was just next door to my photo shop. Everybody there knew me. But why worry? With my store located at the other end of town, it was unlikely that I'd ever run into somebody who knew me.

Anyway, I was wearing a goddamned disguise. My own mother wouldn't have recognized me. But that wasn't the question. The law of averages says that it's almost impossible for you to be standing underneath when a brick falls off the roof. But if it does happen, you can be sure that there's no mathematical law at work. The brick just lands on your head for the fun of it. Likewise, there'll always be a guy — even thousands of miles from nowhere — who comes up to you to shake hands or to pull a gun on you. The son of a bitch knows you. In my business, everything hangs by a single thread — seldom the right one.

After stripping off my beard, removing glasses and cap, I

parked the car across from the Café L'Aube de l'Islam. The Arab bistro had shut its doors five minutes before. I glanced at my watch: it was 11:00 P.M. Suddenly, looking up, I caught sight of a furtive shadow. A man had just emerged from the alley next to the building. Looking around him, he walked down the deserted boulevard, then slid into a gray Simca 1500. The way he disappeared inside the car suggested that he was lying down across the front seat.

A few minutes later, a couple of teen-agers came up the avenue. As soon as they'd passed the Simca, that bastard's head — definitely an Arab's — popped up and watched them go by, then disappeared again. That son of a bitch wasn't sleeping. He was guarding the front of the goddamned café.

The place had been blown up so damned many times that they were being careful now. Unless it was some business involving the rackets.

So there must have been somebody on lookout every night. In other words, that Arab prick saw us every time we went down into the sewers. Could he really have believed we were sewer workers? It's my opinion that he never gave it a second thought. Those guys mind their own business. All the same, it was lucky I'd spotted him.

Two or three minutes later, I caught sight of the Peugeot truck in my rear-view mirror. The driver signaled that he was turning to the left, then parked three cars behind me. As soon as the truck came to a stop, la Fouine jumped out with a MEN WORKING sign in one hand and a steel hook in the other.

I waited until the Arab lookout was busy watching, then crawled out of my car. Because if he knew I was there and on to his number, he'd have become suspicious.

This obstacle course took some time, and when I finally reached the Peugeot, the show was almost over. The whole crew was down in the sewer, and Pierre had his legs halfway down the manhole, when la Fouine, who'd gone along with them, tapped him on the shoulder. They had funny expressions on their faces as they watched me crawl toward them.

I finally straightened up when I got into the shelter of the truck. I explained rapidly that an Arab hiding in a car was watching the Café L'Aube de l'Islam. Pierre immediately jumped back out of the manhole. He wanted to speak to the Arab, but I talked him out of it. It was pointless to get the guy excited — I could imagine myself in the Arab's position. Besides, I told him (and that's why I'd come there) I would return the next morning to pick them up. I'd be parking the Peugeot truck right on the dirt service road near the archways to the right. Now the boys wouldn't need to run any risks scrambling back up the embankment.

At 4:45 the next morning, it was broad daylight again. I did exactly what I'd promised to do. Only one thing went wrong. The service road closest to the archways practically faced police headquarters, and there, emerging in single file from the conduit, were five of the boys, bearded, wearing camouflaged paratroop fatigues as if they'd just fought the goddamned Six-Day War. My fuckin' hair practically stood on end. Shivers went down my goddamned spine. I broke into a cold sweat. I could just imagine some cop glancing out the window on his way to the shithouse. Even if the son of a bitch was half-asleep, his natural impulse would have been to reach for his service revolver and start blazing away.

Laughing, the boys clambered aboard the truck. All we needed was a little background music. I was about to shift into first gear when Biki jumped back out. The son of a bitch hadn't cleaned off his paratroop boots properly and didn't want to track mud into the truck.

"Oh, for Christ's sake, will you get the fuck in! We're parked right across the way from fuckin' police headquarters!"

"You're just pulling my leg," he answered in a voice loud enough for the police to hear.

I shifted into drive. The silence grew so oppressive that it drowned out the noise of the motor.

I wasn't exactly proud of myself for that stunt. From that day on, we always wore the blue coveralls of sewer workers. But we still felt that this place was our best entrance and exit. Only, we never drove the truck down that far again.

Instead, we'd walk along the Paillon from the second footbridge to the archways where we went underground. Our hours might have seemed odd, but no one ever questioned our being there. All the warehouses and workshops of the highway department were located only a few hundred yards away.

CHAPTER 17

The Dark Hours

Friday, May 14, 8:00 P.M.

Eleven guys tumbled out of the truck and headed down the Paillon as far as the archways. It was still daylight. Plenty of people around, especially kids.

"How's it going, boys?"

"Afternoon, messieurs. Don't work too hard."

They knew us by now, for we went through there every evening. We were members of a cleanup crew or else we were exterminating rats — it depended on the day of the week.

"It's about time the city decided to do something down there!" a woman shouted one evening.

God, some people can be really stupid.

We actually became quite cocky down there. In fact, we were often tempted to ask highway department "colleagues" for technical advice.

It was our second weekend in the sewers. The shaft of the tunnel now measured eight feet in length.

We were on the job by ten o'clock each night. We swung into action right away. The stones used to wall up our excavation were stacked neatly to one side. Then we removed the equipment stored inside. The boys would grab their hemp baskets and their wood shorings. Everyone knew his job. All wasted motion had been eliminated.

Sunday, May 16

By Sunday morning — in other words, after thirty consecutive hours of drilling — the shaft was ten feet long. Naturally, things didn't always go smoothly. We ran into plenty of snags. Very early in the game, we had to make a tough choice. Should we drill through rocky soil, or reroute the shaft slightly to reach a vein of sand? We picked the sand. The trouble was that now the men lugging out the goddamned dirt couldn't keep pace with the tunnelers. (We'd long since given up the Indo-China balance yoke. Too damned cumbersome. I'd come up with that idiotic idea.) After that, the soft sand made our shoring difficult. Vertical timbers needed to be set on horizontal ones laid across the floor of the shaft.

Then we came up against a rock that forced us to make another detour. Later, we struck rock again and had to angle the tunnel toward the surface. If we kept on zigzagging, we'd end up in fuckin' China. But the worst was still to come.

About 10:00 A.M. on Sunday, an enormous rock blocked our route. This one was so huge that we just couldn't go around it. We spent a whole week, the next weekend, and part of the following week drilling through that rock.

The task was overwhelming. I never thought we'd get through it. Four drill bits broke in the first fifteen minutes. What's more, our tunnel didn't have much headroom, so we had to work kneeling or squatting or lying on our backs, wearing safety goggles. The deeper we went, the harder it became to breathe, despite our own ventilation system. The lack of air and the heat thrown off by the camp lanterns caused this situation. The jackhammers sent fragments of stone flying into our faces; the dust lodged in our sinuses.

May 17 marked the first dark hours of our partnership. Morale dropped to zero. The boys no longer believed the job would work. It was too long, too hard, too dangerous. They were thoroughly discouraged. Fights broke out daily. It became increasingly difficult to control our crews.

My adventurers were used to swift, incredibly dangerous assignments. They craved the excitement of snap decisions and immediate results. Instant success or failure. Being beasts of burden just didn't suit them. The days went by and they could see no end in sight. The technical problems kept snowballing.

The men from Marseille had their doubts, but still trusted Pierre. But how much longer could that last?

I'd even begun to doubt myself and my own ideas. It got so bad that on Wednesday I had to inform Pierre that five of my boys had refused to go underground. I was amazed by the reaction. "They don't want to go down? That's all right, we'll take their places."

And that's just what the Marseillais bunch did. It bordered on heroism. Personally, I was in an awkward position. And then, without knowing why, my whole unit showed up for work over the weekend of the 21st to the 23rd.

On Tuesday night, there was a real miracle: the rock gave way — it actually crumbled! And we hit clay, beautiful clay, as greasy and yellow as modeling clay. Sixty-eight and Mick plastered the walls of the gallery with the stuff, cramming it between the beams, plugging holes where water had begun seeping in.

We'd tunneled thirteen feet now, and with each blow of the pick we expected to hit the foundation. We dug and dug like maniacs — but nothing happened. It felt as if we were going *around* the goddamned bank. I started to break out into cold sweats again. And the boys began giving me those nasty looks.

Thursday, May 27, 6:00 P.M.

On Ascension Day, a pick wielded by Mick (our good luck charm) bounced off the reinforced concrete foundation of the Société Générale. The tunnel shaft by now measured exactly twenty feet.

The boys had that "something tangible" they'd needed. They were overjoyed. Everyone came over to hug me, then went diving into the shaft. Each man wanted to "pat" the bank. The rough times we'd had? What rough times? Nobody remembered them now.

"How about the foundation? How thick is it?" somebody asked. Pierre and Bouche d'or exchanged a glance, then nodded in the glare of the camp lanterns, which accentuated their haggard faces.

"It's hard to say. In the old days, when they built something, they built it right. Three feet . . . maybe a little more."

A long discussion followed. Should we drill through the foundation or angle the tunnel downward to avoid it?

It was highly probable that we would find clay along the foundation — in other words, easy going. There was one snag, however: owing to obstructions, the gallery had long since ceased to be horizontal. It angled upward. The low ceiling of our tunnel shaft was probably located three feet under the sidewalk. So we had to dig downward three feet — in other words, make a hole roughly twelve feet long. It wasn't easy working at the bottom of a well nine to twelve feet deep. And then there was the equipment . . . Another hitch: when we did reach the wall of the vault, there was no way of testing for an alarm. On D-Day, we'd be forced to pierce the concrete wall and plunge right in, regardless of the consequences.

But there could be only one answer: tunnel through the wall. That wasn't going to be any cinch. We could guess what it would be like from our experience with rock. That didn't matter — we were all going to give it everything we had. We believed in the job again!

The heist had been planned for the long Whitsunday weekend.

Now, the Whitsunday weekend began on June 4—in other words, in eight days. All the safe-cracking equipment still had to be hauled in: blowtorches and about forty tanks of oxyacetylene.

As I had proposed, this gear would be brought in aboard a Land Rover, at the very last minute. I'd already staked out three of these vehicles. Someone would be assigned to stealing one of the Land Rovers the night before or the very night of the break-in. This same vehicle would also be used to carry away the gold, because we'd undoubtedly have tons of the stuff. To cope with this, we'd also acquired a GMC cargo trailer that could be towed by the Land Rover.

Entering the tunnel would be easy, as I had loosened the bolts on the fence rails. You just had to breathe on them and they'd fall away.

We set to work tunneling through the foundation, the last wall separating us from an immense treasure. We worked furiously, frenziedly. But that only seemed to make the going harder. On Whitsunday we were still only partway through the foundation. This underground wall, more than fifty years old, was tougher than Hitler's Atlantic Wall. Each stone of this impenetrable blockhouse was embedded in reinforced concrete harder than granite. Two fifteen-ton pneumatic jacks, a thirty-ton hydraulic jack, and at least one hundred drill bits met their doom in this struggle.

In addition, the bank wall carried the sound of the hammering and made it impossible for us to work continuously. As soon as a pedestrian came near, the lookout tapped the microphone of the walkie-talkie with his fingernail. When our man blew into the microphone twice, we could resume work. A few minutes later, he'd tap again. And so on.

There was also the night watchman and cleaning men. Often, we could work only three hours a night. Once, the cleaning crew didn't leave the bank until 3:00 A.M. We even suspected they were on to us.

Another time, a carload of cops spent part of a night camping right over our heads. They set up this same stake-out three nights in a row. Then they failed to come around anymore, and the newspapers announced a roundup of pimps and whores.

Through the grapevine, we picked this up: "The Paris antigang brigade has landed in Nice. They're supposed to be working on the biggest caper of the century." There couldn't be two biggest capers of the century — not both at the same time, at least. All tunneling came to an abrupt halt. We scattered and lay low.

To our relief, two reliable sources informed us that "the caper of the century" involved the shipment of stolen cars from France into Italy.

Oddly enough, most of the guys who'd wanted to give up only a few days before were now bursting with enthusiasm. The arrival of the antigang squad had done the trick. The boys were solidly united. Shoulder to shoulder. The job was a beauty, and they all believed in it. They'd dig till doomsday, if necessary. The tougher the wall, the more united they grew.

CHAPTER 18

We Won't Use Our Guns

IT WAS AFTER the antigang squad alert that Bouche d'or got his brilliant idea. Everybody was dead set against it. "What? You expect us to go in *bare?*"

Little by little the idea filtered through, penetrating even the most firmly closed minds. Then it was decided officially: we wouldn't be carrying guns inside the bank. We knew the sewers well enough. Two canisters of tear gas would be enough to cover our retreat if we ran into the police.

At the café one noon, while the drilling was in process, I learned that Charlotte had been taken to the hospital. I went over to see her right away. She'd been admitted to the general ward. I took a chair and sat down at her bedside. I'd brought her a bottle of orange juice.

"You can't drink too much, lady," a fat nurse growled.

It made me sick to hear that. I'd barely had time to say hello to her.

"How are you, Bert?" she asked tenderly.

"You're the one who's supposed to be answering that question," I replied stupidly. Somehow, I didn't need to talk to her. She took hold of my hand. It made her happy just to have me there.

"I knew you'd come," she said, while the attendants pushed noisy metal wagons down the aisle between the beds. She kept on staring at me.

"Is it serious?" I asked her.

"The first time I set eyes on you, I wondered if you weren't an idiot. I wonder if I wasn't right," she said with a smile.

Two days later, when I showed up with another bottle of orange juice, the chief nurse told me, as she passed me in the corridor, "She's under morphine."

I went into the ward. They had put a screen around her bed. That meant she was dying. I started blubbering like a baby. She took my hand as usual. Having come to the end of her life, that was all she had.

"It's all set — I'm going out tomorrow," she murmured in a voice that was nearly inaudible.

Her eyes were glazed from the morphine, but I had the feeling that they were searching mine. I don't think her eyes sought compassion or love, but only a reason, a meaning. Because I couldn't answer, she tried to smile.

In a few days, it would be spring. The hills would be ablaze with flowers and fruit . . .

An hour or so later, I walked into a little café. I don't remember what I ordered, but I recall that there was a guy who wouldn't stop talking.

"No, no. She wants a glass of grenadine. If you let her have her way, she'll drink the whole bottle!" Then, a minute later: "The next day, it's the doctor. That's just how she is, I swear to God. You give her steak and mashed potatoes and damned if she doesn't want blood sausage! If you give her blood sausage, she wants pizza. Anyway, if I get angry, she goes into a fit and makes herself throw up. And does she ever throw up! The stubborn slut! She throws up . . ."

And life goes on. It's as though nothing has changed.

Down below, the boys had given up the gravel island in the underground bed of the Paillon River. Now they preferred to use the vast sewer under the avenue Jean-Médecin. That was an intelligent move; it put them closer to their work.

Despite approaching summer, the draft was as icy there as it had been on the underground river, so we always kept a fire burning and the boys came over to dry out. On weekends, le Vieux used to heat up soup or coffee over the campfire, and the shift that was resting would read the newspaper or talk. Le Tombeur managed to get us a little transistor radio. "Maladie d'amour," the old Henri Salvador song, was the hit of the summer.

The weekends and the nights went by. Then, on the night of June 24, after costing us hundreds of drill bits, the bank wall gave way. The reinforced concrete had put up one hell of a stiff fight, resisting all five feet of the way.

We still had another wall ahead of us — the one around the vault. It couldn't have measured more than a foot in thickness, but it was protecting forty million francs. We kissed it.

Was there an alarm? It wouldn't be long till we found out.

But our pent-up emotions burst like a dam. We were deliriously happy. As soon as you lay your hands on cash, you start making plans. Greed actually spoils a good part of the pleasure. But this was the best moment, now that we knew it hadn't been a dream, that we hadn't toiled in vain, that for once we hadn't been wrong, that luck had been with us and anything was possible.

Once our first excitement had subsided, we gathered in the Jean-Médecin sewer to taste le Vieux's soup. We sat around a merry campfire, laughing, telling jokes. Billions of francs danced in eyes that sparkled with joy. For most of the bunch, that money simply meant wealth; for others, like me, it was the thrill of pulling off a big job.

After a while, the fire died out. We had no more wood. It was 11:00 P.M. Zero hour. We got to our feet. Once again, the men's faces showed determination; their movements became feverish. Each wore an apprehensive look now that the moment of truth was at hand.

Indian file, we headed back down the trail. Not a a word, not a murmur, only the splashing of our boots in the sewage. We approached the entrance of our shaft. Gigi and Mathieu stood lookout up on the surface over our very heads. I took the walkie-talkie and called Gigi to ask him to put a bugging device inside one of the vents that supplied air to the vault.

"Put it as far back inside the vent as you can," I told him.

A few minutes later the diaphragm of the walkie-talkie began to vibrate. "That does it!"

I switched on the little receiver that was tuned to the frequency of the bug. Next, I turned the volume all the way up. Then I looked at Pierre and the others. You could hear only the beating of our hearts. Some of them had crossed their fingers for luck. We stood staring at that receiver as though it were a time bomb. If there was some kind of seismic or ultrasonic alarm inside the vault, it would go off like a siren, and that would be the end of our dreams. It would mean a stampede, every man for himself.

I gave Sixty-eight a little nod, and he dove into the shaft at once. Biki followed him halfway through, stationing himself up there to relay my instructions to Sixty-eight.

We'd been in the sewers nine weeks now. Actually, I'd been on the job for five months. If the damned thing ever failed . . . I grabbed the walkie-talkie. "Can we start in?" I asked.

"All clear."

That was all we needed to know. I nodded in Biki's direction, and he raised his arm. Almost at once, the thundering of the jackhammer echoed under the tunnel ceiling. Every man had his eyes glued to the radio. No one moved a muscle.

The only sound that emerged from the radio was the echo of the jackhammer that thundered in the vault.

I gave another nod, which was instantly transmitted by Biki. There was silence once more.

"If there were a seismic or ultrasonic on that wall, it would have gone off long ago," Bouche d'or declared, making a visible effort to contain his joy.

A few seconds went by. The intensity of the experiment had put everyone under great strain. Now the boys traded knowing looks; they elbowed one another in the ribs. Some were actually rubbing their hands.

"How many million francs did you say?" exulted le Vieux, shaking me like he'd shake an apple tree.

I smiled, but knew that it was still too soon to celebrate. Pierre knew it, too, and began to explain the problem while I put the radio away. "A seismic alarm, or vibration detector, isn't always hooked up to a fire gong. Sometimes it's relayed to the night watchman's place or straight to the police station."

"So then what?" inquired le Tombeur.

Pierre was in the midst of lighting a cigarette. They were all hanging on his words. I was the one who answered. "It won't be long till we find out."

I picked up the walkie-talkie again. "Hello, is there a light on in the watchman's house?"

"Yes, but he still hasn't gone to bed."

"You didn't see him go out on the balcony or onto the street, did you?"

"No."

"Start your motor and cruise around the block a couple of times. And keep your eyes open. I'll call you back in fifteen minutes. If you see the cops, don't call — just scratch the microphone. Over and out."

The waiting began. There were twelve of us, and all twelve pulled out cigarettes. As soon as we'd finish one, we'd light another. Fifteen minutes can be a long time when you're counting the seconds. Especially when you're over forty and you just sit around daydreaming all the time.

"Come in."

"Yes. We rode up and down every street in the neighborhood. Nothing unusual."

"Are you parked in sight of the bank?"

"Yes."

"Stay in constant touch and keep an eye on the flashing indicator. Otherwise, you'll screw up the same as you did the day before yesterday. Over and out."

"Hey!"

"What is it?"

"What the hell did you hammer with a minute ago — a pile-driver or something?"

"Why?"

"*Why!* Because you can hear the noise clear out on the street, that's why!"

"Hang on, we're going to test it out again."

Sixty-eight headed back into the gallery.

"Hammer the way you usually do!" I yelled to him.

A few seconds later, we could hear the jackhammers pounding the way they "usually" do under the tunnel ceiling. It didn't seem any louder than usual to us; we'd grown accustomed to it. But Mathieu's voice came over the walkie-talkie at once. "Stop! Stop! You're waking up the whole neighborhood!"

"What the hell is going on? We didn't hammer any harder than usual."

"Hold it. Gigi's going right next to the bank. Now he's coming back. He says that you're hammering against concrete, and the noise is coming up to the surface through the air vents in the vault. The sound carries all over the goddamned building."

"All right. Over and out."

Again we pulled out the packs of cigarettes. If we couldn't use the jackhammer anymore, what could we use?

An electric drill was the only answer. Only how could we power the son of a bitch?

What we needed was a small generator. I had one.

We made our decision. Once more, we piled the equipment in the gallery. While the masons were bricking up the tunnel entrance, I called the two lookouts, asking them to come and get us. Meanwhile, to satisfy Pierre, Rico calculated the amount of wire we'd need to tap the fluorescent light in the garage under the place Masséna.

The answer was five hundred yards. And five hundred yards of waterproof wire, plus three boosters, weighed roughly three hundred and thirty goddamned pounds.

CHAPTER 19

Things Start to Move

Friday, June 25

A long weekend was beginning. Maybe the last. We'd brought down two electric drills, as well as a brand-new Honda 2.5-kilowatt generator. It was supposed to be the quietest model on the market. Then there was a 300-pound reel of waterproof wire that Mick and le Tombeur had dragged through the underground obstacle course.

11:00 P.M.

We were all set!

Contact!

I yanked the starter cord. The generator puttered for a few seconds, then roared. It was running. But the son of a bitch started a goddamned earthquake! I quickly shoved in the choke button to stop the machine. It made more fuckin' racket than ten jackhammers. More noise than a seismic alarm. Christ, I thought the whole damned tunnel was caving in on our heads. Verdict: the generator had to go.

Our only hope now was the fluorescent light in the place Masséna underground garage. Luckily for me, I had refrained from criticizing Pierre's suggestion.

All we had to do was string five hundred feet of cable through the muck, then tap into the current. At first, I thought this installation job would take the better part of the night. Actually, it took only two hours. La Fouine made the connection, and the damned thing actually worked.

So we started right in on the wall with the electric drill. For the rest, we used the pickax and miner's bar. Our tunneling work stopped whenever the walkie-talkie sounded the alert.

The lookout was in position and the radio remained on at all times. That was the wisest plan. The wall of the vault might be crisscrossed with trip wires. All we had to do was sever one of those sons of bitches while drilling and — wham! the goddamned air-raid siren would start. Or else there might be a volumetric alarm, but there'd be absolutely no way of telling that until we'd pierced the concrete.

In any event, this final wall — aside from the fact that it carried the sound of our drilling — would be mere child's play compared to what we'd already experienced.

Saturday, 9:00 A.M.

The drill bit plunged in up to the chuck. That was it! We'd pierced the wall. The last obstacle had yielded. The small hole became bigger.

By 1:00 P.M. the opening was big enough for a man to climb through. That's merely a figure of speech, for we still faced the rear of the huge safe that housed the individual safe-deposit boxes.

But we were on our way. And now we knew for a fact that there wasn't any alarm. Not a single goddamned alarm! The millions of francs sat there waiting for us. They were as good as ours.

Once more, the boys crowded into the tunnel shaft. Guys piled on top of one another like in a fuckin' barroom brawl. They went wild with joy. Their childlike wonder had vanished. Hope had suddenly become certainty. Behind these smiles, each man was calculating his share of the haul.

From here on, Pierre took charge of everything. Operation Open Doors was his baby. First, he'd have to preach a sermon. The gospel according to the boss. In those days came Pierre, the boss, speaking unto them in parables . . . The liturgy of the blowtorch . . . The ascension. It was decided to pull the heist over the weekend of Friday, July 2, to Monday, July 5. Pierre hath spoken . . .

And things started to move.

6:00 P.M.

When the phone rang, I was in the bathroom snipping the hairs in my nostrils. Pierre wanted to see me. Pierre hath spoken . . .

9:00 P.M., at the villa

Couldn't I lend Mireille to them for a day or two? Those guys couldn't have been having any problems with their air supply! "Mireille isn't mine," I explained; "she's *ours.*" All I could do was lend them my share, if I had any time with her coming to me.

Sunday, June 27, 12:15 A.M.

Le Vieux and I crawled under the wire-mesh fence surrounding the used-car lot. Actually, the dealer specialized in trailers and campers. A few yards away from us stood the Land Rover we were going to steal.

1:30 A.M.

Drove to the villa in the stolen Land Rover. There, we loaded as many oxygen tanks as it could hold — about thirty. The vehicle groaned under the weight.

Le Vieux thought he had a brilliant idea. "What do you say we hook on the trailer? That way we could carry the rest of the cylinders."

"You'd better have your name changed if you're going to keep on making stupid suggestions like that. Otherwise, you'll get a reputation."

2:50 A.M.

Thirty-five minutes after leaving the villa, we drove up the boulevard Jean-Baptiste-Vérani to the second railway bridge. A few yards farther, we switched off the headlights and turned left onto the hard-packed dirt road that led to the banks of the Paillon. Then we turned again to get onto the level area. We had to go downhill cautiously when the road became rock-strewn. We were far too heavily laden. The oxygen tanks slid around, rattling each time we hit a pothole. But there was no moon that night. I couldn't see a thing.

Finally, we reached the water and began moving toward the Palais des Expositions. Jolting over the stones, the Land Rover crawled through the ravine so slowly that every one of us broke out in a cold sweat. I kept glancing nervously at police headquarters and had to fight the urge to floor the gas pedal. I swear to God we were right in front of the Nice police barracks. Now le Vieux looked at me.

"I don't suppose you could step on it a little?"

This stretch along the dry riverbed seemed to take forever. Actually, it was only five hundred yards. Five hundred yards at three miles per hour. That makes a six-minute trip. To me, it felt as endless as a walk through a minefield on a foggy night.

All of a sudden the third archway loomed up; it was the only one that had headroom enough for the Land Rover. I pointed the car at the very center of the arch and waited for it to reach us. According to plan, Sixty-eight and Rico had removed the barrier rails.

Oh, Christ, thank God! We were inside the tunnel! I drove another fifty yards before switching on the headlights. Now we could speed up a little. But not much, for each time we hit a pothole it felt like we'd broken the rear shock absorber.

Suddenly there was a tremendous explosion, a blast so deafening that I thought the whole damned truck had blown up. But it was just a blow-out in our right rear tire.

Changing goddamned tires on an overloaded vehicle when you're stranded in a riverbed isn't exactly my idea of a picnic. That night, the two of us had to do it.

3:20 A.M.

Reached the mouth of the Félix-Faure culvert. The whole gang stood waiting for us on the gravel island. There was something new: an inflatable yellow-and-blue dinghy. That was Sixty-eight's idea.

We unloaded the tanks of oxyacetylene, and forty-five minutes later I drove back, empty, to hide the Land Rover at the villa of the Marseillais. During this time, the boys were slinging the cylinders of gas into our tunnel. Naturally, the tanks couldn't all be stacked inside, so we had to risk hiding some of them in different spots around the sewer.

Biki stayed down there to keep an eye on our things. He'd volunteered. In fact, he decided to stay near the tunnel entrance all week. He asked only that food be brought down every day.

After that, there was a week's vacation for all the rest of us. Our next meeting was scheduled for Friday, 10:00 P.M., *in the tunnel.*

The Marseillais, who just couldn't go on living without women, left the villa for greener pastures. They also left all the housekeeping to Bouche d'or, but he accepted it with a smile. Because he knew that Mireille would be coming back from vacation on Thursday. As the day of her return approached, the villa took on its usual smell of dirty underwear.

Meanwhile, at the apartment, we sunned ourselves and admired our Mireille, who spent whole days parading around half-naked. Topless or bottomless, depending on the time or her mood.

Then, all of a sudden, I started to think things over. It was the Marseillais and their attitude that made me think. They'd be happy if there were only five million francs. I'd picked this up just from watching them. By Tuesday, I couldn't take it anymore. I had to be alone.

I went back up to The Wild Geese. Audi wasn't home. She must have been working. That actually suited me better. I was in a lousy mood. I felt positive that something was wrong. The heist just wasn't going to work. Those son-of-a-bitching Marseillais simply weren't cut out for a huge assignment like this. People in the underworld can be tough, hardworking, even reckless. But, unlike adventurers, they're seldom dreamers. To them, every job is the same. They don't give a damn about pulling the perfect crime.

How could such a brilliant plan have gone wrong? First of all, these guys just weren't too bright. Cracking four thousand safe-deposit boxes with three blowtorches, working nonstop for fifty hours — that meant opening one box every forty-five seconds. That was fuckin' impossible.

Christ, why hadn't I trusted the instinct that told me to prepare the flatirons, those expanding devices. With those "nut-crackers" we'd have a chance. Now it was just too late. We didn't even have a diamond-tipped drill. But that really wasn't anybody's fault. Powering a 400-watt electric drill wasn't any problem. But we couldn't use a 1200-watt machine without running the risk of short-circuiting every fuckin' thing in the neighborhood. It was driving me crazy.

I needed to sleep if I wanted to get my strength back, to be in shape. I didn't have the right to resign myself to any god-damned defeat. There was always hope.

It wasn't even 6:00 P.M. when I hit the sack. I was really trying to avoid Audi, for she would have asked me a million questions about that so-called trip of mine. I couldn't face all those lies that evening. Like a coward, I took two sleeping pills, just to make sure I wouldn't be awake. Before falling asleep, I thought about Mireille; about Audi, my wife; about my dogs; about that half-empty house; about the children's laughter that would never disturb my slumber . . .

The next day, the sun was scarcely up when I pulled Audi toward the mountain. She dragged her feet, arguing that she had to be at work. I had to push, coax, wheedle.

The first thing I'd seen that morning was her smile. How wonderful. She'd brought me coffee in bed and just smiled, without asking any questions at all. I was happy to be back with her. Much happier than I'd ever imagined.

I started to kiss her all over. I'd never wanted her as much as I wanted her then. And just as I was about to fill her with my love, she said, "Bert, you mustn't take me for a fool."

I didn't take her for a fool. Was it all my fault if things hadn't clicked? Yes, it was my fault, she said. All my fault. Then she blew up. It had to happen. And lots of angry things were said.

That's the way it happens when two people live together. When two people love each other and put up with each other. We're always destroying something or other. Generally, it isn't for the fun of it; it's simply that we haven't found any other solution.

I knew I'd be making a mistake to say anything. And I knew I'd also be making a mistake if I *didn't* say anything. But I chose the second possibility and continued up the mountain by myself.

Later, when I came back down, Audi had left for work.

I found a note on the kitchen table: "I suppose that you'll be going away again now that we've had this fight. Please feed the dogs before you leave. Don't bother trying to think up excuses — I won't believe you."

Great way to rest up for the big push!

I stayed at Bézaudun for two days. I couldn't take any more than that — I had too much on my mind.

On Thursday, I got back to the apartment. It was like another world: everybody glad to see me, the place flooded with sunlight and laughter.

Joking, Rico dragged me to the kitchen, where Mireille was preparing Biki's lunch pail. She grabbed me right away. "Bert, use your authority. Tell Rico to take me down to the sewer with him. I'm sure Biki needs me. I swear to you. *Te assicura que a besogna di me.*"

"How do you know?"

"Because I know — that's all!" She shrugged, then threw herself into the arms of the other Spanish bozo.

Personally, I had nothing against the idea of her going. I just asked Rico to bring her back afterward. I didn't like the idea of her staying in the sewers.

A few hours later, Rico carried her piggyback through the

meandering underground conduits. And they reached Biki in the Jean-Médecin main sewer.

There, they ate and drank together. But a strange mood came over them. Apparently, Mireille and Biki never exchanged a word but simply stared at each other in fascination. Then, all of a sudden, Biki dropped his lunch pail and began beating on an empty jerry can, as if it were a tom-tom, while Mireille rose to her feet like a sleepwalker. She did a kind of belly dance as she pulled off her clothes.

According to Rico, the tension became unbearable. There was something hypnotic, almost frightening, about the two of them. Rico got up and decided to wait for Mireille on the island of the Paillon. And wait there as long as necessary.

"That girl was really weird, dancing that way, barefoot in the sewage. I had the feeling that I was intruding on some kind of ritual," Rico told me.

Then, he explained, he'd stopped in the Félix-Faure culvert to roll a cigarette. Looking over his shoulder, he'd seen them — stark naked — playing hide-and-seek in the slimy conduits of the sewer. Rico kept going but bumped into them again — this time, actually rolling around in the stinking muck. Locked in a fierce embrace, they moaned in ecstasy. Their cries of pleasure echoed as far as the vaulted ceilings of the Paillon. Apparently, that bestial game in the filth lasted for hours.

"You won't believe me, but somehow it all seemed clean and innocent," Rico told me a few hours afterward.

CHAPTER 20

The Cavern of Ali Baba

Friday, July 2, 10:00 P.M.

On our island in the underground river, the three new men made wry faces as the overpowering stench of sewage struck their nostrils. Pierre had brought reinforcements from Marseille. Maybe things were going to work out better than I'd expected, after all.

One of them, René, had just been released from the hospital (after a beating he got from some truck drivers). His buddy was fresh out of jail. They were both members of our gang who'd run into mishaps back in the days when we'd been gathering equipment. Now they were returning to their regular places. The other two recruits, Honoré and Samy, were professional safecrackers. A skinny little Jew who came from a family in the jewelry business, Samy was supposed to be an expert appraiser. Meanwhile, Honoré held the European record for the greatest number of jewelry-shop heists.

Pierre, la Fouine, and Bouche d'or had been there since 5:00 P.M. Assisted by Biki, they'd already strung the four hundred and ten yards of electrical wire and given it the juice. The entrance of our shaft had also been cleared of its brickwork, and the oxyacetylene cylinders stood at attention along the tunnel walls.

11:00 P.M.

We noticed that the wall of the vault wasn't quite parallel with the back of the safe. The distance between wall and safe seemed to increase gradually as you moved toward the ceiling. This didn't make matters any easier for the Marseillais, who had decided to caulk the space so that the smoke from the blowtorch wouldn't go up the air vents.

That son-of-a-bitching blowtorch! I was dead set against it.

Our first dispute arose. Pierre wanted to extend the shaft and tunnel right through the safe. I contended that we could push the safe over with a powerful jack.

"That's impossible — the safe weighs at least fifty tons. I'm sure that it runs the length of the wall."

"Come on, wise up. You must be crazy if you think they built the goddamned safe while they were building the bank. I'm telling you that they've just got some standard safes standing side by side."

"All right, what can we lose? Let's give it a try."

I tried it — kind of timidly. The jack slid over the metal, making it impossible to get a good purchase. But the safe did move a fraction of an inch. At least, it wasn't exactly in its original position anymore. It became almost impossible to tell how much the safe had moved, for the caulking compound we'd packed into the dead space was running all over the place. It was a real mess.

"All right, enough! Stop it. If you move the safe without being sure you can go all the way, we've had it. There's absolutely no way of putting it back into place. We're going to do it my way: we start drilling into the armor plate right now, and if there isn't enough time left, we postpone the operation for next weekend. At least, using my method, we don't give our position away."

Admittedly, he had a point there.

Saturday, July 3, 12:30 A.M.

The Marseillais caulked the space between the wall and the back of the safe. Next, they hooked up an oxyacetylene torch for Pierre, who began to cut an opening eighteen inches in diameter in the first sheet of armor plating. Right behind that, sandwiched between the first and second layers of steel, we ran into the hardest concrete in the world.

It knocked everybody for a goddamned loop. Even Honoré.

"What the hell is *that?*" he asked in bewilderment.

We held a conference.

Time was running out. We had to make a decision — and fast!

The oxygen lance!

Of course, the oxygen lance — that was the only answer for an obstacle like this. But we'd decided to ship ours back to Marseille earlier in the week, along with other "unnecessary" equipment.

"I've got two of them up at my place."

"Get going! We'll wait for you."

They were going to wait for me, all right. Bézaudun was twenty miles away. What's more, I had to get the oxygen lances without waking up Audi. I needed somebody to go with me.

No luck. Pierre picked le Vieux.

2:30 A.M.

Le Vieux and I clambered up the embankment bordering the Palais des Expositions. The 4L was parked on the avenue du Maréchal-Lyautey. I drove on the way up there. We crossed

Nice, the Promenade des Anglais, then went through the sub-
urbs: Cagnes, Saint-Paul, Vence. After that, twelve miles of
mountain road. Then, Coursegoules, Bézaudun; finally, my private road. I won't go into the details of burglarizing my own
home. I'll just say that it took some acrobatics. I had good cause
for worrying: whenever she was alone at night, Audi got a little
trigger happy.

Anyway, we grabbed the lances and started back. Le Vieux
got behind the wheel — there was no way to talk him out of it.
He knew that we were carrying a precious cargo and that we
had to be careful. He said he'd be careful. Naturally, he immediately began passing every other car. To be careful, he had
to have a clear field. "Too many idiots on the road on weekends," he explained.

One thing was certain: at the speed he drove, nobody was
going to overtake him. We didn't go down the mountain
— we *fell* down. When that madman le Vieux is driving, even
Saint-Christophe (on my medal) covers his eyes. I clung to the
dashboard and kept thinking, Oh, Jesus, I've cheated death so
many times and now I'm going to wind up dying in a goddamned traffic accident on a country road like some asshole
hick!

As we reached the place Masséna in Nice, the air was shat-
tered by a strident whistle. Oh, Christ. For fifteen minutes, I'd
been watching for the cops. Christ almighty.

He was a big fat cop. The whole boulevard shook under his
ponderous bulk. He came up to le Vieux's side and waved
a fat finger under his nose. "If you keep on speeding with
that little van, I'm going to have your license revoked. Got
that?"

"Yes, officer."

"Get the hell out of here before I lose my temper!"

I would have laughed if he'd asked le Vieux to show his identity papers.

Back in the tunnel at 5:30 P.M. Too late — we needed every hour. The heist was postponed to the following weekend.

The trouble was, we'd moved the safe ever so slightly. We decided to keep the bank under surveillance night and day, to be ready for the slightest alert. Furthermore, Pierre stayed at the apartment with us to take an active part in the watch. The others went back to Marseille.

Keeping the bank under observation was fine. But I wanted to see the safe with my own eyes, regardless of the warnings everyone gave me. Monday at 2:00 P.M. I showed up at the bank. I'd worn my Sunday best for the occasion. I walked into the high-ceilinged lobby with its marbled walls. The tall casement windows cast the shadow of a Cross on the marble floor, making the place as solemn as a cathedral.

I went through the usual formalities and was admitted to the stairway that led to the vault. I entered the enormous armored gateway. My heart was in my mouth. Not because I saw anything unusual. No, everything seemed to be in order. I looked and looked, even squinted, but all the safes were perfectly aligned. That's why my heart was in my mouth.

We'd fuckin' well moved a safe; I was sure of it. Not much — maybe an eighth of an inch. So just what the hell was going on? How come I couldn't see it? There was something awfully peculiar about that.

It was good news for Pierre. The fact that the safes were in line meant that there had to be several of them. We could use the jack after all. As for the rest, I must have dreamed it: the safe hadn't moved.

No, I hadn't dreamed it. I was so obsessed that I got the urge to go down that very night and see for myself. Pierre didn't want to reopen the tunnel. He wasn't going to remove all the equipment just to satisfy my whim.

And Pierre said unto them . . .

So I had to go all week in that state of anguish. But if I thought I had troubles then, I didn't know what was in store for me. On Thursday, the newspapers announced the arrival of the president of France. He was attending the inauguration ceremony of a new mall. And where should they decide to stick the fuckin' thing? A hundred yards from the bank.

Any presidential visit meant security measures — special agents would be inspecting the nearby buildings, rooftops, and sewers.

Oh, shit!

We headed for the tunnel that very night. We rebuilt the wall at the tunnel mouth. Talk about being meticulous! And when I wanted to take a peek inside to see the safe, they flatly refused. Nothing doing. They didn't have the time to move all the equipment. Furthermore, we had to find better hiding places for the gear that couldn't fit into the shaft.

And Pierre said unto them . . .

Pierre was right; I didn't try to argue the point.

The last straw was a strike of department-store clerks at Galeries Lafayette. The bastards decided to demonstrate on the day of the mall inauguration. And Galeries Lafayette was the bank's largest weekend customer. Those assholes were going to gyp us out of at least fifty million francs.

The situation was critical. Being a photographer, I had already covered a good many official ceremonies for the local newspapers. I asked around. I tried to wangle an assignment. "Hello, Spaggiari speaking. You remember me, right?"

"Yes, but we haven't made any definite plans as yet. You'll have to wait."

But we couldn't wait. We had to make up our minds: we decided we couldn't risk being in the sewers on the day of the president's visit. We postponed the heist for a week.

All the plagues of Egypt had fallen on our house.

By Saturday morning there was official confirmation: the President of the Republic would not be coming to Nice. We were too far into the weekend — too late for us to change our minds.

"But we've got to take a look in the tunnel shaft just the same — might be seepage or a cave-in."

I had no trouble this time. They gave me the go-ahead signal. That safe was still preying on my mind.

"I've got some fine mahogany planking left. Even some carpeting. It would go great in the shaft."

Pierre thought I was off my rocker. He just couldn't understand these fine points. But my team understood. So we were allowed to go underground to put some finishing touches on our tunnel.

We didn't waste any time: we made straight for the safe.

Son of a bitch, I'd been right! The safe had moved! Only one possible explanation: the safe had been out of line and we'd actually pushed it into its proper position. I have to admit that this sounded pretty far-fetched.

Friday, July 16, 9:30 P.M.

René, Rico, and le Vieux, on lookout at the corner of the rue Deloye and the rue de l'Hôtel-des-Postes, gave us the go-ahead over the walkie-talkie: "All clear!"

We'd been on the job since 8:00 P.M. and weren't planning to use the oxygen lance. As soon as I notified Pierre that we were dealing with a row of safes, he phoned the Marseillais to ask them to bring a thirty-ton jack. In other words, we'd gone back to my original idea of pushing the safe aside to clear a passage.

I set the jack in the upper left-hand corner, where the space between the wall and the back of the safe grew widest. But this time I made sure to jam a wooden wedge between the jack and the metal to prevent the jack's slipping.

Pierre worked the ratchet — once, twice, three times. The boys up front gave a running commentary for those of us who stood in the rear. The safe refused to budge. The stress on the hydraulic jack was increasing. It became hard to work the ratchet. Pierre had to grit his teeth. Five cranks, six . . . The safe groaned as something ripped free near the ceiling. Seven cranks, eight . . . The huge mass of steel began leaning forward, responding to each stroke of the lever. We'd extended the screw of the jack to its limit, so we knocked in wedges to hold what we'd gained. Then we removed the jack and set it higher up. But that was no use: the safe refused to move across the floor. If we kept this up, we'd only strip the thread on the jack.

Time out.

Honoré came up. He was the expert. Like that guy they call in from Texas every time something goes wrong in a French oil well. "Just keep tipping it over," he said, after a moment's reflection.

We set the jack up high again. Honoré worked the lever. He cranked and cranked, tipping the safe over a fraction of an inch at a time, very gradually.

The idea was to tilt the safe enough to allow us to get a man through, but not enough to send the enormous block of steel crashing to the floor.

"Stop!" cried Honoré. He was the one at the jack lever, so he had no trouble obtaining satisfaction.

We hammered in a succession of wedges. And then the jack was removed.

An oppressive silence fell over us. Honoré, Samy, and the other new guy looked at us uncomprehendingly. For a few seconds, everything came to a stop, even time. And those three men kept staring at us. They didn't know what we'd been through to get there. I don't mean the backbreaking toil involved in tunneling, but, rather, the endless doubt and despair we'd had to overcome to reach that fissure between the wall and the thick armor, that narrow opening which would take us to the place none of us had really expected to reach: Ali Baba's cave.

Then le Vieux came crawling through, knocking everyone else aside. He raised his head alongside my knee.

"Forty million?"

"Maybe more," I whispered in a choked voice.

He struck the ground with both hands and kept on nodding.

"Just two million and I go into retirement!"

Now everybody began talking about the plans they had for the money.

Pierre, beside me, wiped his face as he looked me up and down.

"What about you? Now that we're here, haven't you changed your mind?"

"No, I don't care about money. I'm just in it for the satisfaction of pulling a big job."

He shook his head skeptically as he put away his handkerchief.

"All this work — just to give your share away?"

"You wouldn't understand. You have your reasons, I have mine."

"All right. Who goes in first?"

"I'll toss you. Tails, I go first."

He fished a coin from his pocket and, with a snap of his thumb, sent it spinning into the air. The coin rolled between the foundation wall and Honoré's knee.

It was heads.

And again the gallery was plunged into an oppressive silence.

Pierre brought one foot down on the coin while he swung the other one through the gap in the two walls. His expression was serious, his features taut. He began to work his way through the triangular opening with infinite caution, holding the extension light at arm's length before him. He was usually so carefree that we were surprised by the serious expression on his face. He looked like a devout worshiper setting foot in some holy sanctuary.

Next, I slipped through the narrow gap. I have no recollection of what I thought at that exact moment. I was merely a robot.

A second or two later, I was inside the bank . . .

Inside the bank!

Pierre shone his light on the gleaming steel of the safes. No royal palace in the world could possibly hold so much wealth, so much power. Behind the vault's thick armor plating lay a treasure room filled with gold and diamonds.

I'd hit the jackpot! I'd finally won! Billions of men walking around with that same daydream — only this time my number had come up! I'd struck it rich!

Pierre spread his arms expansively. "I told you I'd get you into this room!" he declared.

Me, I could remember how they'd threatened to slit my throat if there were alarms. That's all I remembered. But I was so happy just then that I didn't give a damn about what he was saying. A wave of pleasure flooded my brain. All of a sudden, everybody was there, crowding into the vault. We all hugged

one another like brothers. We pinched ourselves; we turned
around and around; we waltzed. The guys grinned from ear to
ear, their eyes were full of tears . . . And we kept on going
around and around like sleepwalkers. It was too much! We still
weren't sure of anything. We racked our brains trying to prove
to ourselves that it wasn't all just a dream.

I pinch you, you pinch me, we all pinch each other.

The only one out of step was Honoré. He poked around the
safe-deposit boxes looking like a plumber who's about to give
you some bad news.

None of the technicalities registered on me until a few minutes later, when I returned to my senses. Then I realized that
we hadn't broken into the room where my safe-deposit box was
located. (Actually, as I learned a bit later in the night, we were
standing in the first of three separate rooms that made up the
vault.) I'd been incredibly lucky. With the hit-or-miss way I'd
calculated, our tunnel might just as easily have come out in the
men's room.

I stood there while the gang swung into the active phase of
the operation and began soundlessly passing in equipment.

Honoré called for two 4-by-4-inch timbers. He propped the
first under the handle of the safe we'd pushed over. I don't know
what he did with the other beam — I was too busy extending
the folding ladder so that Biki could unscrew the metal lat-
ticework connecting the top of each safe with the ceiling.

He tore off part of this grill and saw that it would be unnecessary to caulk the ducts, which had openings on the street. First
of all, this would have been far too complicated. Second, these
ducts meandered so much that the glow of the blowtorch
couldn't possibly be seen outside. As for the smoke, there were
enough air vents to carry it away without attracting attention.

On the other hand, what did require immediate caulking was
the thickly armored door giving access to the basement of the

bank. Since that big son of a bitch was located in the other room, Rico and Gigi began cutting through the door that separated us from that room. It was a tempered-glass door backed by a steel grating. They needed to saw through only a few bars. Another two-man team set to work tearing the carpeting off the vault floor so that the stuff wouldn't catch fire.

A chain of hands passed in equipment continuously.

Meanwhile, Pierre readied his blowtorch with the assistance of Honoré, who kept offering advice. Pierre flatly refused to take any. The flame was adjusted so badly that he could hardly cut his way through the metal around the lock on one safe. Later on, during the investigation, an expert from Fichet, the manufacturers, spoke about "a blowtorch virtuoso." If only that guy could have seen what really happened! As Honoré kept saying over and over, Pierre just wasn't aiming right. He'd bring the goddamned torch so close to the fuckin' metal that his flame would get snuffed out. I guess he was in a frenzy. Actually, he had forty-eight hours of burning ahead of him, so his technique improved tremendously. But that particular door kept him sweating for a solid hour. It was just one plate of steel after another and, sandwiched between them, a thick layer of refractory cement. All of which adds up to a real pain in the ass, because the expansion of the materials traps a lot of heat. This extinguishes the torch flame, touching off a chain of little explosions.

All our blowtorch specialists watched him very carefully, because they would be choosing a system on the basis of Pierre's experience with that safe and one individual safe-deposit box.

Pierre finally cut out a circle large enough to reveal a portion of the lock mechanism. After he did some groping and prying with a jimmy, the double doors swung open.

The safe contained fifty safe-deposit boxes. Pierre immediately set to work burning the hinges off one of them. No results. Next, he cut the hasp from top to bottom. But the molten metal and expansion jammed the lock better than a good weld. It took powerful blows with a sledge — and with a crowbar after that — to break in that stubborn door.

The result was disappointing: nothing inside but a sheaf of old papers.

We spent a long time examining that safe-deposit box because there would be nearly four thousand more, each identical to the first. We were up against steel an eighth of an inch thick. No problem with the hinges — two shots with the blowtorch or, if necessary, the electric saw. After that, we ran into a snag: the hasp came down over the front of the box. It had to be cut off before we could pull the box out.

This was far from the ideal system. We knew about a more efficient method some pros were using, but that would have required a power source we didn't have. There was no current anywhere in the vault. All we had was the electricity we'd brought in from the garage under the place Masséna.

Five "torch artists" tackled a safe door apiece while Pierre wrestled with his second safe-deposit box. During this time, I experimented with another method. Using a piece of cardboard, I traced a design of the riveting on the remains of the first box. Next, I tried to melt the rivets with the blowtorch. A big waste of time. I dropped that idea fast.

Finally, we decided on this technique: we'd cut off hinges and hasp, then smash in the bottom of each compartment with a sledge. That would twist the whole thing out of shape. Next, we'd slip a jimmy into one of the cracks and pry the door open.

We tried it, but it took forever. We'd never make it at that rate.

I tried another idea: ripping the whole compartment apart

with the hydraulic jack. But the jack wasn't in line with the floor and the base of the safe. Another failure.

Damn it! I should never have gotten myself mixed up with that fuckin' bunch of amateurs! Why couldn't they have brought me a two-hundred-ton jack instead of that thirty-ton piece of shit?

And what about a gooseneck adapter for the jack piston? With one of those sons of bitches, we could have cracked the safes like matchboxes.

Next time, Bert. Next time . . .

Now the vault turned into a beehive of activity. Every man worked feverishly.

Samy was the only one twiddling his thumbs. He just sat at the table like he was waiting for his laundry to dry. When I gave him a surprised look, he replied calmly, "Appraisal and sorting of jewelry. Nothing else. Appraisal and sorting — that was the agreement with Pierre."

Then he looked at his fingernails. Something about his face made me want to scream.

Shortly after midnight, we finished sawing through the gratings that separated us from the other rooms of the vault. We were through the tempered-glass door, as well. Biki immediately caulked the thick double doors with clay from our own tunnel so that no smoke could escape into the bank. And one man took up position right next to the door, in permanent radio contact with the lookouts on the surface. A second walkie-talkie operator stood guard at the far end of the tunnel.

Saturday, July 17, 4:00 P.M.

The heat became infernal. All the boys were stripped to the waist. They'd been working for eighteen hours straight.

Morale was high, but fatigue and stress began to make themselves felt, despite the Dexedrine pills. To top this off, we realized that there wasn't going to be enough water. Fewer than thirty safe-deposit boxes had been opened. The pickings were slim. After the astonishing success of the first phase, it looked like the heist would turn into a fiasco.

The whole wonderful job had been ruined — by sheer negligence. I hadn't had enough money to engineer the job by myself. So when it came to picking my associates, I hadn't had any choice. "He wasted his life because he didn't have any choice." What an epitaph. For some time, I'd known that these boys just didn't have the class for a job of this size. Only, what else could I do? I'd realized my mistake too late. I couldn't have backed out. But quite honestly, I'd often thought that it would all work out in the end, that maybe I was just imagining things, that I was probably just a worrier.

Now I had to watch them struggling with the safe-deposit boxes.

Only a stinking twenty-eight boxes opened! Oh, Christ! According to our schedule they should have cracked fifteen hundred of the goddamned things. It was still possible. It was still possible — that's what drove me nuts. I thought about Marcel, the most clever burglar in Europe; about Gilbert the blacksmith; about little Pierre; about fat Michel; about all those Italian outfits. Christ, with any one of them we could have busted more than a thousand boxes in eighteen hours.

I had to get out of there. I had to breathe. There was no water — I'd go get them some. Anyway, it was all arranged for me to leave so that I could construct an alibi for myself. Nice was my territory; everybody else came from out of town. I made my way through the sewers and trudged upriver to the Palais des Expositions. Damn it! Carelessly, I'd awakened an Arab derelict. To eliminate all worry, I bawled him out in German. A few yards farther, the sunlight smacked me in the face. An old man was washing his car, but he was so wrapped up in his high gloss that he never noticed me.

I walked quickly to my car and drove straight to the apartment to take a bath and get an hour's shuteye.

According to instructions, Mireille woke me up at 6:00 A.M. with a mug of coffee and buttered bread. Then she began pacing up and down, naked as a jaybird, in the glare that filtered through the rattan blinds. Now she was always naked. Stripped for action: that was her motto.

"How's it going, down there?" she asked timidly, wringing her hands behind her back. Suddenly she looked like a little girl who'd made a wish.

I reached out, groping for the night table, where I'd put my cigars. She quickly snatched up the lighter and held it for me.

"You look unhappy, Bert."

Sometimes a disappointment can be even worse than actual disaster. Like packing your bags and getting to the pier just as the boat pulls out. Watching a boat leave port from your living room window isn't so bad. But when you're standing on the goddamned dock with your suitcase, that's another matter entirely. I've seen that happen plenty of times.

I raised myself on one elbow to sip my coffee. Then I threw back the covers, got out of bed, and started to dress.

"How come you don't want to talk to me? Tell me what's going on, for God's sake!"

"I had a fifty-fifty chance of pulling this job off. Well, I screwed up. Get dressed. I'll come and pick you up in a little while."

A few minutes later, I was speeding toward the Route de Marseille, toward my photo store. The manager didn't close it until 7:00 P.M. on Saturdays. When I got there, I "handled" some customers. I made a point of giving them lots of advice; I actually demonstrated the use of the cameras. In those fifteen minutes, I did more talking than I'd done in the past few years. At least, it seemed that way to me.

Constructing an alibi was a hell of a lot harder than you might think. Sometimes months elapse between the date covered by your alibi and the date on which the police come around investigating. By then, you practically need an affidavit signed by a court clerk if you expect your alibi to stand up. Just try asking somebody to swear that he actually spoke to you on a Tuesday at 4:00 P.M. three months ago. Especially when it isn't you but the police doing the asking.

That's why I had to leave an indelible impression in the minds of those customers.

It was Charlotte's saint's day, God rest her soul. How she would have enjoyed coming to my rescue.

I crossed the highway and entered the café. I announced that I was standing everyone to a round of drinks in honor of Sainte-Charlotte's Day. Okay, everybody on your feet. Here's to Sainte-Charlotte. "Charlotte?" somebody mumbled. "I used to be in love with a girl named Charlotte." Ah, cut the crap, for Christ's sake. Let's go, everybody. On your feet. *Vive Sainte-Charlotte!* Come on, François; give everyone another one of the same. It was going to take a while before any of them forgot that.

Next, I bought two six-packs of Evian water and went back to the apartment to pick up Mireille.

We had supper on the avenue Félix-Faure . . . right over the heads of our pals, real or otherwise.

CHAPTER 21

No Hate, No Violence, No Guns!

Saturday, July 17, 10:00 P.M.

The situation had changed. In the past six hours, thirty more boxes had been opened. What was more, they proved "fatter" than the first ones. It looked like the boys were improving.

The cash, gold, and jewels were beginning to pile up. The operation wasn't going to be anywhere near as big as I'd expected. There was still a chance, however. If things kept up this way, we'd go down in the annals of crime with the robbery of the Glasgow-London mail train.

We were young and hard as nails. Come on, at those steel boxes! Smashing, tearing, prying, our crowbars and jimmies never stopped.

All those drinks to celebrate Sainte-Charlotte's Day had blurred my vision. I'd joined the festivities for a good part of the night.

There was something almost orgasmic about cracking a box. It was like catching a big fish or raising the lid of a Spanish treasure chest. As soon as the guy with the crowbar shouted, "I've got it!" we'd all lunge forward to plunder the mysterious treasure he'd unearthed.

Samy, the little Jew seated comfortably at his table, sorted the gold and silver. His thin fingers manipulated the jewelry and precious stones with unbelievable dexterity. I swear, the guy could have swiped the false teeth from a chow dog without getting bitten.

"This ruby? No, that's a waste of time. Too hard to fence, too easy to spot."

That ruby just happened to be insured for six million francs. I apologize to the charming lady who wasn't robbed. I'm sure that you were terribly disappointed. But honest, lady, there was no slight intended. You may rest assured that we'll notify you of our next robbery. We'll split it fifty-fifty; what do you say?

Samy had two knapsacks and two satchels. He'd just toss the leavings — like that ruby — onto the floor. Jewels in settings went into one of the packs; unset gems and pearls went into the other. He put the gold and platinum into the two satchels. He collected more than six hundred pounds of the stuff.

Mathieu, a lover of paper, went through all the envelopes, classifying secret contracts, marriages, illegitimate promotions, fraudulent agreements, blackmail letters. For any enterprising thief, these papers alone represented a regular gold mine, a swindler's Fort Knox. And Mathieu sorted. He put the wills to one side, made piles of stocks and bonds. There were mountains of the goddamned things. We just didn't have time, bags, or arms enough for that. So it was all left on the vault floor.

Bouche d'or, who had managed to get his foot under a falling steel door, stayed at the radio and did all our cooking. He was the one who called our attention to the night depository. Businessmen who worked late or stayed open during the weekend could drop their day's receipts into the bank, through a slot on the rue de l'Hôtel-des-Postes.

"They keep dropping the damned stuff in. You'd better have a look at it."

"All right, we'll take care of that in a while."

Fifteen minutes later: "Say Pierre, what about that depository?"

Half an hour later: "Jesus Christ, I can't stand it anymore. I'm going to have a goddamned stroke. Are you going to do something about that slot or not, damn it! They keep dropping in their deposits."

Finally, Honoré got to work on it. He was an artist with the blowtorch. It took him less than twenty minutes to crack that door. The basket inside was full of bags containing the receipts from the Casino supermarket chain, as well as the main department stores, like Prisunic, Rapides Côte d'Azur, Manufrance, Nouvelles Galeries. We cut open some bags, and there was a regular cascade of banknotes. At a guess, more than ten million francs.

Sunday, 4:00 A.M.

Eight safes opened so far. In them, about one hundred and seventy safe-deposit boxes had been emptied. The assembly-line boys, dropping with fatigue, went on smashing like beasts of burden. It was paying off now. Only, the guys couldn't keep going like that. I'd seriously misjudged their endurance.

I remembered the time when I'd had the Viets breathing down my neck. I'd had to keep moving for days and nights without sleep. That's what the gang was trying to do now.

"Let go. One more before we go to bed!" And a little later: "All right, this one is the last!" Half an hour later: "God damn it, I'm not going home without busting that one."

Their hearts may have been in the right place, but they were so bushed that it was a waste of time. Somehow, they had to get some rest.

Right from the start, I'd suggested that they take mild amphetamines to keep them going. But none of the boys from Marseille would touch the stuff.

Those hoods just couldn't stay on their feet anymore. So they started taking two-hour naps on a rotation basis. Then we had to replace the three lookouts at street level. Nobody wanted to volunteer. It would have been damned near inhuman to appoint a man arbitrarily, so we drew straws. It was decided that only two lookouts would stay on duty until Monday morning. Biki and Hervé drew the short straws.

I'd begun making bundles of cash. Seven bags full. I gave Biki and Hervé each a bag of banknotes. I had no trouble finding four volunteers to carry the rest. The guys were half-dead from asphyxiation, so the walk did them good.

We started on our way, seven men and seven bags. Through the sewers, the Paillon River. Every one of us knew that mile and a quarter like the palm of his hand.

We emerged on the streets of Nice in the middle of a downpour.

After loading our haul in one of the two cars, we covered everything with old flowerpots. Biki and Hervé took the VW Kombi, which was parked on the avenue du Maréchal-Lyautey. The other boys went back underground with me.

The water in the sewers hadn't risen yet, but we would have to watch out.

8:00 A.M.

His clothes creased and dusty as if he'd been crawling under a house, le Vieux came up to the stove to pour himself a mug of coffee. "I'd say we're close to the seventy-million-franc mark. Goodnight, boys." And he returned to the theater of operations with the haste of a man who's parked his car in a bad spot.

Ten minutes later, Pierre and I were prying open the pair

of big strongboxes that stood in the last room. In the first one, nothing. In the second, three million francs, the bank's reserves.

"Say, this bag is kind of light, isn't it?" grumbled le Tombeur, who'd come to carry away the bags of money.

"You guys could try a little harder than that," added his sidekick, la Fouine.

In the second room there was a row of separate strongboxes, without armored doors to protect them from greedy hands.

For some purely personal reason, Pierre chose to tackle the strongboxes in the first room. No doubt he imagined that the biggest bundles must be hidden behind the thickest armor plate. Having no such prejudices, Rico and I began cracking one of the safe-deposit boxes. We found the most beautiful collection of jade imaginable. Ask Samy; he knows.

On the other hand, the second box was full of food: coffee, chocolate, and cookies. For the most part, the goddamned stuff was moldy. We decided to try one more before giving up. But we'd begun to think that Pierre had the right idea. That's when we came across a diamond necklace worth four million francs. We were hot now; we didn't want to quit. In the next box lay a ring with a twenty-carat diamond; in the others, a flood of jewels, gold ingots, and coins.

It turned out that this room, although much more lightly defended than the other, held a far greater treasure. This we learned too late.

On top of that, we kept hearing more and more profanity from the next room, each time the Marseillais ran into boxes of cigars, collections of cheese labels, nudist magazines. Either that or safe-deposit boxes in which some middle-aged woman was saving her husband's dirty pictures. And then some stupid son of a bitch would be keeping a box full of sugar and lentils.

Gigi and Carlos began pasting up pornographic pictures on the compartments facing the vault door.

Near this main door we'd set up our dormitory, dining room, kitchen, and latrine. There was no shortage of food, what with the tins of liver paste, fancy sausage, smoked ham, crates of fruit. "Byzantine," as one reporter later described our tastes. On the other hand, the wine was downright awful. Margnat Village! It was Bouche d'or who bought that damned swill. What an asshole! Why didn't he buy Postillon or some shit like that while he was at it? But I've got to admit that he did cook us some amazingly good soup.

He'd set up his battery of butane stoves between the walkie-talkie (located where we got the best radio reception) and our latrine.

It should be pointed out that odors had long since ceased to bother us. Even Honoré, who'd come prepared with spray cans full of pine scent, was now sleeping alongside the golden tureen in which le Tombeur had just taken a crap.

10:00 A.M.

One of the lookouts on the street warned us that the watch-man had just entered the bank. Blowtorches were snuffed out at once. The torch artists seized this opportunity to catch up on their beauty sleep. Meanwhile, Rico and Carlos took turns keeping their ears glued to the vault door. Mick monitored the sleepers for possible loud snoring.

Except for those three, plus Sixty-eight and myself guarding the money bags, everyone else was asleep.

Cylinders of oxyacetylene, rubber hoses, blowtorches, crow-bars, sledges, cold chisels littered the floor, along with dis-carded jewelry, stocks and bonds, cigarette butts, empty wine bottles, canvas bags, and twisted steel wreckage. There was something unreal about the sight, like looking at hand grenades with no pins.

Samy slept at the table, with his head buried in his arms, while Sixty-eight and I stood back to back, our elbows interlocked, swinging each other back and forth hard enough to crack our spines.

Around 11:00 A.M., we inspected the sewers. The water had risen about twelve inches.

12:00 noon

Mimile, the watchman, had just been seen leaving the bank. There was a wild scramble. Action stations! Man those blowtorches, those crowbars, those sledgehammers! The vault was soon full of acrid, asphyxiating smoke, with the temperature close to ninety degrees. Our frantic activity resumed amid the hissing of blowtorches. The boys moved like sleepwalkers, hair plastered with sweat, trousers slipping down, bare torsos streaked with grime. Some lost a good deal of weight in the two days and three nights. But the millionaire sewer workers were getting fed up now. They kept looking at their watches. None of them had ever seen so much money in his life. They had more than enough. A few of the boys even kept track of the number of boxes we'd cracked, as if it were some kind of feat.

Me, I was just counting the ones that remained untouched. Damn it, there were thousands of those sons of bitches. What a goddamned waste!

Every dream has to come to an end. And mine had ended the day before. I'd find another dream to spur me to new heights, but, for the moment, I was like the rest of them, out on my feet. The pep pills I'd been taking weren't even working anymore.

As night drew near, the output dropped to half. Even a Hercules like Mick was exhausted.

12:00 midnight

We began packing up the rest of the haul. The load was heavy, bulky. Even though there were sixteen of us, some men — the strongest — would have to make several trips. No so for the equipment. Right from the start, we'd planned to leave it behind.

We cracked our last safe-deposit box at 1:04 A.M. It was our three hundred and seventh.

That's all, folks!

From that moment on, the boys were magically transformed. Blackened faces, swollen with fatigue, suddenly brightened. A carnival atmosphere reigned. There were gales of laughter. Me, too; I couldn't help laughing. It was from nervous fatigue. We could hardly stay on our feet. We looked like some kind of goddamned scarecrows; but I just kept on laughing.

The men who'd gone into the heist for the money would come away wealthy men. The rest, adventurers like myself, were happy, too. It was the largest sum ever stolen.

We'd pulled *le fric-frac du siècle,* the heist of the century!

Pierre still hadn't shut off his blowtorch, so he used the flame to weld the armored door shut. It would take the bank officials longer to find out about the burglary. At first, they'd think it was simply a malfunction of the lock mechanism. That had happened before. In such cases, they always summoned experts from the manufacturers, Fichet. Only this time, they'd have to drill, and that would take hours.

Meanwhile, the boys were trying to come up with a suitable slogan to scrawl on the bulletin board that faced the vault door.

One guy suggested, WE WISH TO EXTEND OUR SINCEREST THANKS TO THE MANAGEMENT. Another offered, INTEREST-ING WORK IN PLEASANT SURROUNDINGS.

After fifteen minutes of this horseplay, we decided on NO HATE, NO VIOLENCE, NO GUNS!

This was going to be the first thing that the manager and the head teller would see, smack in the middle of a wall papered with every dirty picture we'd found in the safe-deposit boxes. The bank officers were almost sure to recognize customers in that collection of photos.

I could just imagine how it would go: "Good morning, monsieur. Yes, it's awful, all right. Your safe-deposit box? Let me check my list. Naturally, they've taken all the negotiable banking papers . . . Ahem, ahem! . . . But there were some photos . . . ahem . . . and certain papers . . . They're bound to be in this drawer . . . I must admit that I haven't even had time to glance at them . . . Ahem, if you'd be so kind . . . Ahem, I mean, if you don't mind, I'll be leaving now. I must . . ."

What a farce!

We took a final precaution before leaving the vault: Sixty-eight and Carlos emptied the fire extinguishers over places where ungloved hands might have left fingerprints.

CHAPTER 22

The Flood

Monday, July 19, 2:00 A.M.

We put on our street clothes while Bouche d'or distributed an advance of twenty thousand francs to each man. The sum was intended to cover any accident on the way back.

Immediately afterward, a human chain began passing the heavy loot from the vault into our tunnel. La Fouine, meanwhile, took one last look around the vault — to make sure we hadn't forgotten anything. He finally emerged with one of the big camp lanterns.

"Everything's okay," he announced.

Two days later, I read in the newspapers that a pack of one hundred 500-franc notes had been overlooked. Fifty thousand francs left behind! All right, that isn't so much. I just mention this bungling because it's typical of the job as a whole. Well, the second phase of the job, anyhow. In other words, the actual robbery. Because the tunneling has been acclaimed by experts everywhere as a masterpiece.

Our loot was crammed into knapsacks and army packs. We staggered under the weight of jewels, gold coins, and ingots. Each man's pack was geared to his strength, loads ranging anywhere from sixty to one hundred and twenty pounds. The only exception was Samy, who carried the precious stones. His small pack weighed less than twenty-five pounds.

Nine packs were left over.

The men who weren't returning took a last look at the tunnel. Our caravan lurched forward.

The trek was brutal. An icy wind hit us as soon as we emerged from the vault's stifling heat. In our weariness, the weight of the packs seemed doubled.

Just as I'd feared, the level of the water had risen considerably. Bent double under their loads, the gang picked their way through the current, clambering painfully over obstacles. The swirling water reached our thighs, but we were managing all right until the Chauvain main sewer. Then the going got so rough that our column bogged down.

First of all, there was la Fouine. He flatly refused to go on. I wedged my own pack behind a drainage pipe and waded up to the head of our column. I could understand the man's reluctance about venturing into the swift current of the main sewer — the water might be shoulder-deep. But we had to come up with an answer. Pierre also moved up to the column's point. Together, we studied the situation. Obviously, the water wasn't as deep on the walkways, but they were terribly narrow. With our heavy loads, it would be dangerous to use them.

Finally, Mick, our strongman, took the bail of the lantern in his teeth and plunged into the murky water, his pack held over his head. As soon as he reached the deepest point, Mick's hand shot out. He managed to keep his balance by clinging to a pipe. Chest-deep in water, Mick's hundred and ninety pounds of bone and muscle weren't enough to buck the current. Naturally, his pack had gotten wet. Before we finished, all our packs were soaked, and most of the approval certificates on the gold ingots had become illegible.

How the hell were we going to get out of that sewer?

Mick told me that he could make it without his pack. So I asked Rico to go back and get the coils of rope we'd left in the vault. I had to shout to make myself heard over the noise of the swift-flowing sewer.

And then we waited, our teeth chattering, while torrents of sewage poured through the tunnels of the underground city. Few things scare me, but the rising waters in that sewer did. The boys wedged their packs against the walls as best they could. No one spoke. We kept playing the beams of our flashlights over the depth gauge.

At last Rico returned. We tied the ropes end to end. Mick volunteered to secure the end of the long rope to some pipe at the next intersection of the main sewer. The rest of the gang could use the rope as a lifeline. That way, we'd work our way from one stretch of sewer to the other until we reached the Paillon River.

I had another idea: go for the inflatable boat we'd left at the gravel island. We'd load the heaviest packs aboard and then tow the son of a bitch. We finally decided to do it.

The boys from Marseille were getting their confidence back. But we had to wait nearly three quarters of an hour for the boat. In other words, it was 3:20 A.M. when we started loading the first six packs aboard. And the first squad plunged into the water, clinging to pipes. Samy couldn't take any more. I barely had time to grab hold of his sleeve. The current was carrying him away like a chip of wood. Sixty-eight and I hauled him onto the walkway and wedged him in a niche. He'd already lost his flashlight. He was pale and trembling. "I refuse . . ." he kept mumbling. I took his little pack, and le Tombeur slung him over one shoulder. And off we went.

4:05 A.M.

We'd reached the little island in the Paillon. We were completely exhausted. Wiped out. Yet, almost at once, six volunteers started back into the subterranean torrent: Sixty-eight, Gigi, Mick, Rico, Carlos, and le Tombeur. It took real balls to go back in there, no matter how much money was at stake.

By now, we were already an hour behind our most pessimistic forecasts. Outside, daybreak was approaching.

The rest of us set out on the second leg of the trip, a mile and a half of gravel or egg-sized stones under the concrete archways along the river. Here, the waters had scarcely risen.

At the last minute, I'd decided against driving the Land Rover in. It was just a hunch I'd had. For two and a half months, we'd been taking chances, some calculated, others not. Here it was the last day, the day we scored. I didn't want to push our luck. My proposal hadn't exactly got the unanimous approval of the others.

Like inmates of a penal colony, we trudged over the slippery, uneven path. The sacks of gold weighed more than one hundred pounds apiece. By now, their carrying straps had all broken, so it was impossible to get a hold on them. The boys slipped and fell constantly. They hadn't had more than four hours' sleep in three nights and were punchy with fatigue. Then la Fouine took a bad spill, landing right on the point of his spine. He couldn't even get back up on his feet.

4:45 A.M.

The sun was rising behind the valley of the Lovetta. Biki decided to take a big gamble. He backed the Peugeot right up to the fence where the Paillon went underground. Mathieu watched for cops from the footbridge at the Palais des Expositions. He was behind the wheel of the 4L, so he could create a diversion in case the cops showed up.

With one last effort, we heaved the gold over the tailgate of the truck, then clambered wearily aboard. Hervé had to help la Fouine in. The other guys just stood there, unable to take another step. Even if the cops had come, none of us would have budged.

Pierre and I looked at each other. We were both thinking the same thing: What about the rest of the loot and the other boys? He glanced at his watch; I looked at the bolts that held the two rails of the fence — they hadn't been tightened yet. Next, I looked at the boys. Besides Pierre, only le Vieux and Bouche d'or seemed at all lucid. I signaled to the others, and they piled aboard the Peugeot. They needed no second invitation. Then I explained my plan to the three Marseillais.

Biki would take the truck to the prearranged place and wait there with the boys and the freight. Meanwhile, Pierre and I would go for the Land Rover, which was parked nearby, and drive down the tunnel as far as our island. At the same time, le Vieux and Bouche d'or were to take the two remaining vehicles, the Volkswagen Kombi and the Citroën panel truck. One would station himself at the avenue du Maréchal-Lyautey; the other at the boulevard Jean-Baptiste-Vérani. In other words, one on each side of the Paillon. Like Mathieu, they were to stand by, ready to create a diversion.

A few minutes later, the fence rails were down and the Peugeot truck started off. So did Bouche d'or and le Vieux.

At 5:20 A.M. the Land Rover was jolting its way down the riverbed. Our three other vehicles stood at their posts. The rain had stopped, but the city streets were still wet. Aside from this fact, I was too stupefied with fatigue to notice anything but the riverbed, which disappeared under the front end of my car inch by inch. Four minutes later we slid under the concrete archway.

I switched on my headlights and fed more gas. A couple of hundred yards farther in, I heard a whistle and jammed on the brakes. I quickly made a U-turn. Rico, Carlos, and le Tombeur, who had dived for cover at the approach of the car, stood blinking in the twin beams of the headlights. They were lugging five sacks. Pierre and I loaded the freight and men aboard. Then we turned the Land Rover around once more and headed for our island.

Sixty-eight, Gigi, and Mick still hadn't returned from their last run. Rico and Carlos got out to fill the knapsack they'd left behind on the island. The pack of cigarettes in the car passed from hand to hand.

My watch showed 5:55 A.M. The three passengers in back were snoring. Pierre was dozing. I chain-smoked to keep myself awake.

At 6:10, the three boys still weren't back.

Now I figured something had gone wrong. I jumped out and started down the tunnel for the mouth of the sewer. As I was about to enter, Gigi appeared.

"What the hell have you been up to?"

"One of the sacks broke, damn it!"

"Did you lose the stuff?"

"No, we brought it all back. But it wasn't any fuckin' picnic," Sixty-eight replied for him.

I knew damned well they'd been through an ordeal. Backs bent double, the trio, sodden and filthy, emerged from the culvert. They straightened up as best they could, the muddy bags at their feet. I don't remember exactly how it happened, but suddenly we were all hugging each other. Maybe we even started bawling.

PART THREE

TRAVELS, JAIL, ESCAPE

CHAPTER 23

Bigger than the British Mail Train Robbery

GIGI TOOK OFF without waiting for the split. The twenty thousand was enough for him. Destination: South Africa, where his services as a fighting man had already been retained. The other members of our unit disappeared four days later. I never found out what use they planned to make of their money. All I know is that they weren't attracted to a life of ease or sensual pleasure. War was their bag.

Mireille and le Tombeur left together.

The party was over.

The first night, all eighteen of us had celebrated. The second night, after the split, we had another party — this time, among ourselves. We'd gone through some unforgettable experiences. We drank to them before each man went his separate way. Some of us would never meet again; that was certain. Danger was too much a part of our lives.

And then one morning, there I was, alone in front of a cup of black coffee, in the bar at the Nice airport.

The caper had caused quite a stir. On Tuesday, the *Nice-Matin* ran banner headlines: SENSATIONAL BURGLARY AT NICE BANK. By the following day the wire services had told the story all over the world (my boys sent me press clippings from every continent) and the *Nice-Matin* splashed the news over the whole front page — COLOSSAL BANK ROBBERY — and devoted three pages to the story. Paris reporters and cops came flocking south by the trainload. The newspapers were unanimous: "Bigger than the British mail train robbery."

On July 24, the Société Générale offered a million-franc reward for information leading to the capture of the robbers. They'd put a $200,000 price on my head. Really big-time stuff.

The apartment had been rented to the end of the month, so I stayed on a few days. I needed to be alone. It felt strange, being all by myself in that big place with no other souvenir of the summer than a few boxes of bubble bath. I needed another dream to spur me on. That's what made me linger there.

The beginning of the dream started with a word that had a magic ring: lasers.

With a laser I could have gotten forty million francs in no time at all, with no fuss, no noise, without even getting my hands dirty. There were lasers on the market that I could have used, but they seemed to be shrouded in secrecy. The type I could have adapted to my purposes was called the "torch." It had been developed at an American university. However, the patent was sold almost immediately to the Japanese. Burglary is almost nonexistent in Japan, outlawed by the secret societies, which divide the nation into territories. That's why you can leave a gold ingot on any park bench there and nobody will touch it. So the Japanese had no qualms at all about making this particular laser available to their own fire departments. It's no big deal going to Japan. The tough part is making yourself understood over there, without creating suspicion. They don't even have an underworld, so none of the Nice crowd could possibly refer me to a friend over there. That laser torch went on being a dream, nothing more.

I tried to come up with something more realistic — like a mini–oxygen lance. Then I started feeling like I had some kind of iron band around my head. I hadn't really recovered from my depression. Suddenly, I was overwhelmed by weariness. I hadn't found God in the vaults of the Société Générale. The quest for the Holy Grail continued in the mist-shrouded moors of my defeats.

Before closing my eyes, a thought made me laugh bitterly. I recalled a childhood incident. I might have been six years old at the time.

"Sis, do they have movies in heaven?"

"Of course not, silly. In heaven, we find bliss in the contemplation of God. The movies are for this world, on earth."

"Aw, damn it!"

I must have gotten one hell of a good beating that night.

On Sunday afternoon, I headed for The Wild Geese. The magazines, the radio, and TV were still talking about the heist of the century. My first euphoria had worn off. The enormous stir created by that lousy, botched-up job of mine left me dumfounded. It was just plain incredible. After digesting all the facts, the reporters simply failed to see that this robbery, executed so brilliantly at first, had ended in a miserable flop. More than thirty-five hundred safe-deposit boxes left intact. Couldn't those idiots understand that? Damn it! Damn it!

I'd just driven through the suburb of Saint-Paul-de-Vence. The motor was purring contentedly in the warmth of the morning sun. In my pocket, two hundred thousand francs. That little bundle meant two or three months of vacationing, travel.

I reached the chalet at about 9:30 A.M. Parka quickly picked up a stone and brought it over to welcome me home. Vespa, wagging her tail frantically, wore a big smile. But Audi was busy tending her flowers and paid no attention to anything else.

As I stooped beside her, she casually turned her head so that I could kiss her cheek. Without so much as looking my way.

"Come on, now. Don't be a sourpuss."

I knew it was pointless to yell at her. I dropped my jacket and walked toward the field. I loved this place to which the rains carried the richest soil of the Chéron. Yet long ago the farmers had abandoned it. Before I bought that property, schoolchildren had played there, sheltered from the winter winds. Only few shepherds, hunters, gatherers of truffles, used to wander through what was left of the sheepfold. And with each passing year the stone walls of the twelfth-century watchtower crumbled a little more.

That tower had guarded the village and the mountainside against the enemy — the Arabs from the valley below. The life of an isolated community had been concentrated in this place. Now, after centuries of communion with the earth, a mere fifty years had sufficed to destroy everything.

When I first stumbled across this spot, it dawned on me that if I ever founded a family and settled down someplace, it would be there. The sheepfold was dilapidated and the property completely overgrown. The farmers made fun of me, and so did the villagers. I did everything all with my own two hands, and it took me years — long, hard years — to turn the place into what it is today. I not only cleared the land, but hauled fifty tons of concrete over a mule path to strengthen those twelfth-century walls.

But as I've said, "Without children, there can be no tribe." The house turned out to be just one more daydream. That castle, that refuge, that eagle's roost, was built for — nothing. None of the children that I might have had would ever ride out to plunder the lowlands and fertilize the mountainside.

A few days later, I left for Spain, just to stretch my legs a bit.

When I got back — wham! — a fence that worked with my friends informed me that a certain Francis — the Ectoplasm — had offered him some ingots at a bargain price. "Only, you understand, they're hot. Société Générale stuff."

Oh, my God! In terror, I phoned le Tombeur, the only person I could reach. Four of them were on their way to rub the *mec* out. Meanwhile, I let my feelings get in the way of my judgment. Like an imbecile, I started to plead for that asshole's life. "No, there's nothing to be afraid of — he'll never talk. Even if they arrest him, he knows better than to squeal on us. Besides, where would that get him? He'd just wind up in the clink without making a sou."

"Are you sure?"

"It's only logical, for Christ's sake!"

But it wasn't logical at all, damn it! As I would see later on, the stupid son of a bitch made a full confession.

CHAPTER 24

My Trip and . . . My Arrest

"GET MY STUFF PACKED, sweetheart. I'm going to take a little trip over to see the Rockefellers. Start getting your stuff ready, too. A week from now, I'm taking you to the land of the rising sun."

A few minutes, a few clouds, a few Scotches later — Kennedy Airport, New York. Immigration, rain, Yellow Cabs. I liked the place right away. America is a country that lives its own life, enjoying immense freedom. A country that isn't building much of anything. A country destroying itself and waiting for the Messiah. America is way behind, but also way ahead.

It's a place where absolutely anything can happen. Where kids kill each other — the way European kids fight with their fists — over a smile or a dollar. Where they announce over television that seven hundred New York cops are assaulted each year. Apparently, they bury them in mass graves over there. A place where the queers are manly; the whites black; the blacks nationalists; and the Jews Aryan.

New York, with its three million illegal aliens, its broad avenues potholed worse than any North African *piste,* its ghetto smells, its decrepit, barb-wired taxis. New York! Systematic, generalized madness; grace and ugliness. Freedom flavored with shit. New York isn't the United States — it's just the purgatory of America.

The next morning I got up, with that six-hour time lag, on my own sunrise and had the brilliant idea of sending a post card to Audi. Before I even mailed the damned thing, I managed to get stuck up for a dollar; lose my way in Central Park at night; end up in Harlem, which I crossed on foot; pay fifty dollars for a twenty-dollar room at the Plaza; try French cuisine made in Italy: escargots in linguini.

They say things like that don't happen in other parts of the United States. That's kind of a shame.

American cinema is good because it's more than just realistic. It's real. *Taxi Driver* is no isolated experience, but a daily occurrence. At every other stop, Super Madman crushes some loathsome maggot in a haze of marijuana. Nothing counts; nothing is important. A guy can blow a fortune shooting craps in some lousy basement, then go twenty feet away and beg for a dollar to buy himself something to eat. If his house explodes, he just shrugs and goes on his way.

New York, city of tramps, winos, adventures. The Anglo-Saxon mind. That insane right to complete freedom.

Noise, frenzy, greed, rage, despair, skyscraper and ghetto, wealth and poverty; nothing makes any sense. More than anywhere else, people scream and spit and tear — but they get by.

Those people living in America, in New York City, wage war against world poverty, against all the problems of the under-developed countries. With their dollars, with their blood, they pay for that fundamental law: man is on his own and each of us must bear the responsibility for his own problems.

Hypocrisy is also part of the Anglo-Saxon mind.

America is the land of the pioneers and of the Apocalyse. It

will shape the planet to its own mold or bust everything. So
be it.

I made a hop over to France and whisked Audi away to
Japan. I traded the six-hour time lag for a nine-hour one.
Tokyo, Hong Kong, Bangkok. It's all the same. Nothing excit-
ing. The gods in those countries don't really attract me.

I had the foreboding now that this trip would be my farewell
gift to Audi. She had the foreboding, too. "Now that I'm getting
older, you're going to leave me."

And yet, that October, I loved her more than I had for years.
She returned my love a hundred times over.

"You can go away — I'll wait for you."

For a long time afterward — perhaps for the rest of my life
— I would remember those days we stayed in Japan, just you
and me in that insane crowd.

Just you and me. And a little guy. A cop. That's right. I
wouldn't want the chief of police to take me for some kind of
chump. That cop did a damned good job — don't get me
wrong. He had this kind of out-of-place look, as though he felt
lost among all those veteran diplomats and businessmen. (He
got himself a seat on the same charter flight that I had. Actually, the trip was sponsored by Jacques Médecin, the mayor of
Nice, and intended to promote the Riviera tourist business in
Japan.)

The guy came around crying on my shoulder; he didn't have
any sales contacts. Damn it, that son of a bitch was such a good
actor that, for a few minutes, I almost believed him. But I just
hope that the French courts won't bill me for the expense of
that guy's flight. If you people want to go around tailing us all
over the world, that's your problem, not mine.

Anyway, I got suspicious. Tick-tock, tick-tock . . .

I wasn't part of the Ministry of Tourism's delegation, but I knew several of its members by sight. I'd photographed them for the Nice papers back in the old days. How come they were all ignoring me? I mean, they wouldn't even look my way. Was my imagination playing tricks on me? No, not to that point.

Tick-tock, tick-tock . . .

There was the Nice bank heist and something else. A few months before, I'd agreed to hide a few guns for an extremist group, and, unhappily enough, some clown managed to get himself assassinated in Italy shortly afterward. I learned that on my return from New York. Interpol might have traced it to me; after all, I had a police record and it was anything but impossible.

Tick-tock, tick-tock . . . Doubt and confusion.

I was used to trouble. It's practically always the same. From the first time long ago to the latest right now, trouble impales you on its sword. But you learn to take it in your stride; you gain experience. Rule number one for critical situations: rise to the occasion. Don't allow circumstances to alter your plans, your appearance, or your habits.

Since I'd planned on returning to Nice via Hong Kong and Bangkok, that's exactly what we did. On the evening of October 24 — a Sunday — we landed at the Nice–Côte d'Azur Airport. I had an appointment with my dentist two days later.

On this day the newspapers announced the mass arrest of what the reporters called "the Sewer Gang." I kept my ears and eyes open. More than ever, I sensed trouble. Yet everything around me seemed perfectly calm, like nobody had seen or heard anything.

I didn't trust that calm for a second. I went over the store and the house with a detector, one of those small electronic devices that can spot wire taps and bugs. At my house it reacted positively along a line running through the living room wall. I did some more checking and found that the emission line extended into the atmosphere. It seemed to be coming from the Villeplaine plateau, on the other side of the valley, just across the way from The Wild Geese. It might be remote-controlled by a laser beam — the French intelligence service was equipped with them. Unless, of course, some amateur was responsible. I did have a neighbor over that way who was crazy about electronic gadgets. But why the fuck would he be so interested in my house?

Things were starting to look fishy.

At 6:00 P.M. on Tuesday, October 26, my dentist Lulu handed me the telephone. A voice that was cold, calm, and unfamiliar echoed in the receiver: "I'm a friend. I've got to see you tomorrow. How about two in the afternoon?"

"Which friend?"

"Can't tell you over the phone."

"We could get together right away."

"Look, I'm calling from Lyon. I won't be there till tomorrow. [A silence] It's very important."

"Okay."

I hung up, wondering. Were the police postponing my arrest just to stall for time? Maybe; I couldn't be sure.

But one thing I did know for sure — only two people in the whole world knew my schedule: the dentist and a friend of mine, Jean-Yves. This fellow had gotten into trouble during my trip. A case of fraud involving a bum check. They took him down to the police headquarters but released him after a good tongue-lashing. I'd have the answers to these questions before long.

Meanwhile, I got back into the torture seat, and Lulu resumed his work. After a moment, he switched off his light. "We've still got to match up the color, but I'll do that tomorrow."

What the hell? I had to come back the next day just to match up the color of a goddamned tooth? That couldn't take more than a couple of minutes.

I hope it wasn't you, Lulu. I hope it wasn't you, Jean-Yves.

The next day, I had lunch with Jean-Yves at the little café opposite my store. Actually, he didn't eat anything; he'd just come for a cup of coffee. I talked about this and that, then told him of the phone call I'd received the day before and the meeting I was going to have in a few minutes, outside my store.

"I wonder what the hell it's all about?" I added.

And he thought it sounded funny, too.

Wednesday, October 27, 1:45 P.M.

I just had a snack — a *croque-monsieur.* I got up from the table and went over to drink my second cup of coffee at the bar. I was still debating whether to show up at the meeting or not. As far as the heist was concerned, I wouldn't be running any risk. They'd never come up with the slightest clue. Unless, of course, they concocted a bunch of phony evidence of their own. Cops will do almost anything to make an arrest. I was in the midst of thrashing all this out when a cop entered the café. A pensioned police sergeant, he'd come out of retirement to go back on the force. He lived in the neighborhood, and we knew each other pretty well.

He came over to me with a broad grin and slapped me on the shoulder. "Did you see how we nabbed them — the bunch from the Société Générale job?"

"Hey! Take it easy, will you? Must think I'm some kind of punching bag or something! Nabbed? Who did you nab?"

"Say, you weren't in on that one, were you?"

"You know me better than that. The Charge of the Light Brigade. That's more my cup of tea."

No sooner did I finish my sentence than I spotted my little cop from the flight to Japan. The son of a bitch was trying to pretend he'd just come in to buy a pack of cigarettes, but I saw through his game right away. To top it off, the bungling idiot came over to shake hands.

It was 1:55 P.M. by the clock on the café wall.

Who the hell was this creep? French intelligence? The honorable representative of some Italian secret service? Or an ordinary flatfoot from Police Nationale shadowing me? Yet if that were the case, if I'd been under surveillance for so long, the cops had to have much more on us than they had. How could they keep following blind leads, like their idiotic stake-out on some villa, allegedly the headquarters of the Sewer Gang? The papers talked about a gang from Marseille, but that didn't mean much — any time somebody stuck up a filling station between Perpignan and Menton, the papers always linked it to the Marseille underworld.

Crooks, just like people in finance and entertainment, transact their business via phone and Telex. They travel by jet and use computers to do their bookkeeping, whereas most cops still have to count on their fingers.

But cops are lucky, people say. It's true. And that luck of theirs, when you help it along a little, produces some of the worst miscarriages of justice in the world.

At any rate, they needn't have taken so many precautions — I wasn't even carrying a gun. Proof that I suspected something. Rule number two: don't take unnecessary risks.

2:00 P.M.

Let's go. I left the café and crossed the Route de Marseille, heading for the parking lot in front of my store. When I got there, I noticed a car on my left. Inside sat two men and a woman. The two guys got out, coming my way. A couple of lookalikes. Two of these New Wave dicks. You know, sloppily dressed, long-haired, kind of pale. All of a sudden, they split and whipped out their revolvers. The synchronization was so perfect that they must have rehearsed a million times. But these *mecs* didn't have any brains. They would have got dropped in any western shootout. You never approach a right-handed gunman from the left. I could have dropped those knuckleheads in their tracks if I'd been dodging the police.

"Okay?"

"Okay."

I put my hands up. Then they twisted my arms behind my back and handcuffed me. Only after this did the color return to their cheeks. Next, they paraded me ceremoniously more than a hundred yards, until we'd reached the headquarters of the operation. And then they started coming out of the woodwork. Rats — people who'd put the finger on me. One of the rats was a female. From what I hear, she'd been trailing me since dawn.

I tried to brazen my way out of it; I even blew that dame a kiss. You have to be nice to the underprivileged. And I gave them the false-arrest routine.

Still protesting, I broke out laughing. *"Me?* In on the Société Générale job? Ha! Ha! Ha! Don't make me laugh, inspector! *Me?* In on the . . . Ha! Ha!"

All of a sudden, I stopped my act. I realized that I had a little scrap of paper in my goddamned pocket. With three phone numbers on it! That was the end of my swaggering. I felt like jumping off the nearest bridge. Oh, shit! I'd meant to flush the numbers down the toilet before leaving the café. And then those two asshole cops had to come in. I'd just plain forgotten in the excitement. Three goddamned phone numbers that could turn me into the biggest stool pigeon in history.

CHAPTER 25

The Metal Detector

THEY MADE ME get into their car, my wrists still handcuffed behind me and a couple of big bozos on either side. I was in real trouble. Half an hour later, the motorcade stopped at the end of the avenue du Maréchal-Foch. In front of the Sûreté Nationale headquarters.

They moved me from one place to another. I swear, there must have been fifty of them around me. Kind, understanding, and all that. They kept bombarding me with questions and searching me — all at the same time. Each one wanted to do his bit. It was this oversupply of manpower that saved me. They went through my pockets and even tickled my anus along the way, but somehow they missed that scrap of paper. The strangest part was that they searched me several times. And each time my heart stopped, needlessly. Luck was on my side for once.

An hour of interrogation and filling out forms, and then we headed for The Wild Geese.

The Land Rover was being repaired; it needed a new water pump. As for our other car, Audi was using that, and they still hadn't brought it in. No ordinary car could make it up the mule path leading to the house. So we had to go on foot. One cop thought he was a wise guy and tried to drive his prowl car up there. The numskull got himself stuck. He even needed all the other cops to help get his jalopy back down.

Half an hour later, they were at work. First they went through the motions of searching the house. But they lacked any real conviction. After only five minutes, they started unpacking the metal detectors and made straight for the chicken coop. They didn't give a damn about the workshop, the garage, the metal shed, the gazebo, the fields, or any of the outbuildings. Just the chicken coop.

"As long as you have daylight, you might as well start in there, eh?"

Hahahahahaha!

They ran the metal detectors over the ground in front of the rabbit hutch for a few minutes. Then back to the chicken coop. I swear, my heart stopped beating.

But the metal detectors didn't buzz — not a sound. The son of a bitch was on my side. As I've already said, it really was my lucky day. The machine revealed nothing but nails and rods used for reinforcing concrete. Each time that carpet sweeper passed over my cache of guns without buzzing, I felt like kissing the goddamned thing. But those bastards had nothing else to do, so they started ripping up the fuckin' floor, chasing out my indignant hens. Then they seemed to go berserk. They ripped and smashed everything. When there was nothing left of the chicken coop, they began digging up the beaten earth.

And finally they found what they knew to be there. I mean guns and explosives.

Five years minimum. I made a quick mental calculation. I'd be forty-nine when I . . . I had to laugh all the same when the cops unearthed the arsenal, weapon after weapon, without even remembering to look for fingerprints.

"Watch out! A couple of those things are booby-trapped. If

you touch it wrong, the fuckin' thing blows up in your face."

They froze. None of them dared to pick up another gun.

"You ought to ask that guy who squealed on me — maybe he knows."

"Look, you're in enough damned trouble as it is, Spaggiari. Don't go making matters worse for yourself. You made all that up about the booby traps, right?"

"That's right, I made it all up. Just to throw a scare into you."

Without stool pigeons, there wouldn't be any arrests. The day robbers get together and eliminate all the squealers, the Police Nationale might just as well close up shop. All that business about brilliant deductions and relentless sleuthing — that's a lot of crap straight out of some comic book.

Seriously, aside from open-and-shut cases of petty theft, what good are the cops anyway? The best example is my own heist. With the nation's entire police force called out, it wasn't until then that they got me. Even though I'd been standing there in Nice with a neon sign over my head. The facts are simple enough. I planned that robbery alone and, at the beginning, I didn't believe in it. It was just so colossal that it seemed like a fantasy, nothing more. So I went around telling everyone about it, sort of boasting. But I managed to pull the job off. And everybody in my neighborhood knows that I masterminded the job.

The best part of all is that the cops can go back over Nice with a fine-toothed comb and they'll never find the slightest evidence to incriminate me, directly or indirectly. They can't back up their charges with that lantern they found in our tunnel. Afterward, they came around and planted the damned thing in my house. It's the same stunt they pulled at that villa. Aside from our loot, nothing came out of the sewers or the Paillon. Nothing.

So they had to come up with something else to get the goods on me. And they did come up with it, all right. I have to give them credit for that. I've since learned from an interview in *Minute** that a former member of the OAS informed the police about the arms buried under my chicken coop.

The arsenal had been discovered. From that moment on, I was officially under arrest. My little world began to crumble. But the earth went on revolving, and my trees continued to grow. Did it mean that I was nothing, that I meant nothing to anyone?

"What about your wife?"

My wife was no danger. I'd never informed her about my illicit activities. It was a pact we'd signed long before. As soon as she heard that I'd been caught, she went straight to the Sûreté. They released her a few hours later.

Now they pushed me back into the car. This time we were headed for the interrogation room at police headquarters. I glanced one last time at that place which might have changed my life. That place where I'd been happy for a while. How can you leave things you love, knowing you'll never be back? And I was sure of it already, sure I'd never be back there. I would have to find something else to hang on to.

"Okay, paratrooper, out the door!"

I did as they told me, and, since the handcuffs had been removed, I seized the opportunity to swallow that scrap of paper bearing the three phone numbers. I barely had time to gulp it down when they chained me to Savelli, a decent old cop within months of his retirement. He's a cop from another school.

Now, damn it, I had to count the minutes until 2:00 P.M. on Friday. According to French law, they couldn't grill me longer

---

*Translator's note: a right-wing weekly published in Paris.

than that. And I knew they weren't going to give me a second's rest.

The curtain was going up for the first act. The questions started to fly. At times, ten cops did the asking; at times, it seemed more like fifty. They didn't stop; as soon as one finished, the next began. They made me talk about everything under the sun. Where do you buy your ties? Your shirts? Why are your socks blue? What kind of razor do you use? Their aim was to wear me out. They didn't ask me the real questions until later. They dragged me from one office to the next, from one chair to another. Some of them just split their sides laughing; others spat, screamed, drooled, farted, exploded, spluttered, ate, patted, shook, jumped.

There were red-faced ones, purple-faced ones, pasty-faced ones, sweaty ones, grimy ones. Some of them liked me; others threatened, cursed, flattered me, shook their fists at me. Others talked about electric-shock devices; others about bathtubs. They were trying to get me all mixed up. They were getting me in shape.

But Bertie Spaggiari had been through a few other grillings. I glanced at my watch. "Just thirty-six hours to go!" I yelled. "You coward, you stupid punk, you dirty son of a bitch."

Those are a few run-of-the-mill examples of the abuse heaped on me. I liked to get their goat. I gave it back to them, tit for tat. "Hey, your buddy is shaking like a leaf. Better not leave any matches lying around — he'll burn off his own mustache."

But they were too happy having me in custody to take any chances by beating me up. They knew I was struggling to stay awake. I couldn't even keep my eyes open.

The second act: they'd let me doze off for a few seconds and — wham! they would smack the table with a wooden paddle. Or they'd practically kick my stool out from under me. Other times, they slammed the door as hard as they could or they'd wake me up and lead me into a darker room.

"You'll be more comfortable here."

Wham! The wooden paddle smacked the table. I woke up with a start, blinded by a harsh light.

"Your name and date of birth? Hey, René, you're at the typewriter. Let me see your forms. How many carbons did you make? Speed it up if you can — I've invited my brother-in-law over for supper. Christ, every time he comes over, we really tie one on."

"Hey!"

"What? Oh, yeah, that's right — I forgot about that guy."

Wham! The paddle came down on the table.

"Your name, your age, your address?"

"I didn't do it, officer. I swear, I'm innocent."

"I thought you were smarter than that, Spaggiari — I guess I was wrong. Henri, bring in one of those bozos."

Instantly, I fell asleep. Wham! The paddle hit the table.

I opened an eye. And who do I see in front of me, wearing handcuffs, his face puffy, with a big cop on either side of him? None other than Francis, the Ectoplasm, in person.

"Yes, that's him, officer."

"What do you mean — *him?*"

"Spaggiari, the brains behind the heist. He was the ring-leader. He put me up to it."

Put him up to it! I put him up to it, he said. He was only a grown man. And he let himself be "put up to it." The son of a bitch said it again, swore to it, then burst out into honest-to-goodness tears.

I was wide awake now. As strange as it may seem, I wasn't really sore at him. It just made me a little sick, looking at that weasel. I felt sorry for him more than anything else. I thought to myself, Francis, you stupid fuck, I'd rather take this rap than be in your shoes.

But why the hell did they need a confession from me? Didn't they have the arms cache? That alone was enough to put me on ice for the rest of life. They told me, "We need your confession so that we can wind up this case. Just for the newspapers, you understand."

Inspector B——, a gentleman who knew all the rules and who was prepared to make any sacrifice to observe them, had this to say: "For us, this case is more important than the arms cache. Monsieur Spaggiari, if you help me, I'll help you."

"What do you take me for — some kind of chump?"

"Not at all. Just try me, you'll see."

"My confession in exchange for the arms rap?"

"It's a deal. I can have the arms charge dropped in exchange for your confession."

"Okay. I'll confess to anything you say, only first you kiss my ass!"

Wham! The door slammed. Bye, inspector.

That was just the intermission. The play resumed.

The detectives who were supposed to be nice offered me something to eat. The ones who were supposed to be mean slapped it out of my hands. The same with cigarettes, the same with matches. "No, put it out! The inspector might be back."

Next, they started in on my weak spots: my political views. That isn't a bad way of making a guy lose his temper. But, as I've told you, I'd been through this kind of thing before.

"You guys in the OAS, you were just a bunch of stupid punks." It was Inspector T—— who made that remark. It suited him perfectly — that was just the way he thought. He didn't need the slightest prodding to start spewing his filth. "There was only one pimp — de Gaulle! He buggered you and then you kissed the son of a bitch's ass!" In a rage, he flung his jacket onto the floor. His eyeballs were ready to pop. *"Pieds-noirs,* paratroopers; it's all the same to me. A bunch of fuckin' queers and misfits!"

I was expecting a reaction from one of his colleagues, almost all *pieds-noirs.* Maybe they'd start a fight. No, nothing happened. Most of the detectives just stared at their goddamned shoes. Then the inspector snatched up his jacket, clicked his heels, and went storming out. That little creep is going to blow a gasket someday, watching himself play the role of Hamlet versus the Indians in his full-length mirror.

Audi came into police headquarters of her own accord. (I'd given her instructions to do so if anything ever happened.) Later, I learned that the guy had ranted at her, "When you marry a hood like that, you're no better than he is!"

Then Inspector B —— took over. "Go ahead, Madame Spaggiari, talk! That's what your husband really wants you to do. He'll be relieved. That way, he doesn't lose face."

And then Inspector B —— had this to say to me: "You're a leader, right? Well, act like one!"

"I'm no leader, officer. I swear, I'm innocent!"

"Shut up! Nobody's innocent!"

He was right, but it was fun feeling innocent, like in the good old days.

That goddamned arms cache! Once more I was going to be the victim of a miscarriage of justice, unless they came up with some dirty trick to make me confess.

When you get arrested in France, you've got it made. You know they can't use torture or beatings. You can't be subjected to more than forty-eight hours of questioning. And yet lots of people talk. They squeal on friend and foe alike.

"You're going to get the book thrown at you, whether you

confess or not. And all alone, like a big sap. Those partners of yours won't come to help you. Unless maybe they come and see your widow, bring her flowers — or maybe something else while they're at it."

The cop wasn't lying — that was a tradition of the underworld. The guy who got himself caught had to take it on the chin. He might wind up on the guillotine, but his pals on the outside would never move a muscle for him.

Fewer innocent men would be serving time if it weren't for this underworld rule. There has to be some kind of harmony between the courts and the offenders. Often, justice operates on a system of barter: "We'll clear you of these charges in exchange for the guy who murdered the child." And it's the suckers who pay.

The police can't just go around making all these stories up; everything must be substantiated. That's why they needed my signature. The case had attracted enormous publicity. The cops were really on the spot. Hundreds of reporters stood waiting outside police headquarters, their arms folded, their eyes pitiless, unblinking. The newspapers wouldn't be satisfied with just a few scapegoats. They wanted the leader's head.

All through my interrogation, I realized that the detectives were in close touch with the top brass in Paris. I also realized something else. (Yes, everything was gradually becoming clear.) I'd doubtless been fingered long before, but the police wanted proof positive before arresting me. They were expecting to catch me in some error. When they failed to find one, the police started in on that political crap, hoping to uncover a weak spot. The cops did come up with the arms cache. (The information must have cost them plenty.) They had me. Now what kind of trade-off . . . ? Unfortunately for them, things didn't work out that easily. I wasn't interested in making deals.

The situation was growing desperate for them. They'd used up their whole arsenal of psychological tricks, including a trade-off on the arms rap, and time kept ticking away. They weren't making the slightest headway. Then they turned me over to T ——. Now T ——, he's their ace in the hole. A guy so swamped with work that he does all his sleeping while riding or flying to and from Paris, Marseille, Nice, or Lyon. It seems that he'd spent the night at *police judiciaire* headquarters in Marseille and appeared at the Nice Sûreté Nationale fresh as a daisy. The top brass in Paris were really treating me to the best.

There are three kinds of cops available on the French market:

1. The ones who managed to be on the winning side in '44. Big, fat, and stupid. Living proof that back in those days people thought only of their bellies. These cops ate and drank themselves silly. It certainly wasn't overwork that put the gray hair on their heads.

2. The offspring of the Vichy militia. Beaten from Dakar to Algiers, by way of Mers-el-Kebir and Saigon, but always rallying to the side of an idol. In '58, de Gaulle returned to the scene. It took these Frenchmen only three months to realize that the "great families" had tricked them again. Only, they'd signed up. And when you're a cop and you've signed up, you go to work whether you like it or not.

Chief Inspector T ——, the supercop, belonged to this second type.

"You know, aside from the fact that it was Indo-China for you and Morocco for me, we've been in the same boat — we both believed in what we were fighting for."

My wife had once told me the same thing, but it wasn't true. T —— and I weren't in the same boat. I hadn't needed anybody to kick me in the ass.

Yes, in 1962, I did believe in all that. But not the part about a French Algeria. I'd believed in an Algerian Rhodesia that would tell the mother country where it could get off.

Actually, though, that isn't true. I'd never *really* believed in it. Because if I'd had even an ounce of faith, I would have squeezed the trigger of my Mauser that day in September '61 at Hyères, when I had de Gaulle right in my sights.

3. The last type is the New Wave cop. Their school was May '68. But that one month wasn't enough to make them more mature. A couple of tear-gas grenades and three kicks in the behind made them choose the side doing all the kicking. But the cost of living is high, so they had to pawn their boots. These cops go to expensive hair-stylists; they drink Coca-Cola. They look sexy, not tough.

While T —— and I were chatting, I asked, "But don't they answer the purpose, inspector?"

"We expect them to be able to cope with any situation they're up against. For these extravaganzas that the public seems to want, we always have plenty of clowns who've gone to college. And if we can't find them, we'll make them up. You and guys like you are small potatoes; nowadays, real crime has gone commercial. It's going on way over your head. You'll understand that when you write your book. Because you *will* write one."

What a charmer! T —— made me feel like we were having a friendly conversation over lunch. The atmosphere had changed completely since his arrival. Now the detectives all relaxed. They laughed and talked freely. All we needed was the wine and glasses.

"We'll wear you down, Bert. There are a few excellent reasons why you're going to confess: the arms cache, your wife, our know-how, your image. You pulled the heist of the century, right? You're number one all over the world! Your throne is waiting. Just sit in it and you'll be crowned. The newspapers are just waiting for a signal; then they'll plaster your picture on the front page all over the world. Now, if you refuse to talk and persist in denying everything, you're going to do time for a crummy rap — illegal possession of firearms. A bunch of clowns will claim that they're the brains behind the heist of the century. That'll turn this whole caper into a laughingstock. Now, just between us, Bert, it would surprise me if that was what you wanted."

"It strikes me that if anybody's going to be a laughingstock, it's you!"

"Okay, you get the idea at any rate. Our interests do coincide, and that's just why we've got to talk turkey."

The hours went by, and the interrogation was turning into a real pleasure. I wasn't even sleepy anymore; I'd gotten my second wind, just like in '52, when I'd been in peak condition. But all those detectives looked miserable.

Toward midafternoon on Thursday, T ——— , a good loser, had them bring me an omelette. Oh, was that ever delicious! The best I'd eaten in ages. They also offered something to drink, but this I refused for fear they would slip me some kind of drug. I must have been right because the detective who was holding the glass of wine really blew his stack. Oh, Christ! That made me scared about that damned omelette! If ever I started losing control, I'd knock myself out somehow. I'd bang my head against the corner of a desk.

Now I was offered a smoke. I took it but kept on my toes for some telltale flash or click as I slipped into another world. Absolutely nothing.

"Bert, listen. I don't give a crap about that arms cache. As far as I'm concerned, we never saw those guns, okay? Now here's my deal: you're going to confess and stand trial; there's no getting away from that. Only — and get this — you weren't even armed; there was absolutely no rough stuff. You've got every chance that the court will recommend leniency. You've also got to remember that the robbery never created a negative impact on the public."

Credit where credit is due. You've got to hand it to those boys from the Sûreté. They never stopped trying.

The day went by. Then the evening. Around 3:00 A.M. they were all bushed, out on their feet after forty hours of disappointment. Even T —— was on his last legs. A day-old growth of beard stubbled his face, and two bitter lines had formed at the corners of his mouth. He got to his feet and snapped hoarsely, "Okay, I think that about wraps it up. We've grilled this guy for more than forty hours — we're plain wasting our time with him. Lock him up for the rest of the night. Bring him back tomorrow morning at eight, and we'll go and open his safe-deposit box at the bank. Then we can write up the charges and hand them to the judge."

Wearily, he ran his fingers through his hair, then took a couple of steps my way. "No hard feelings, right, Bert?" he said, like a good sport. Then, with a yawn, he turned to the detectives and asked, "How about a little coffee before you turn in?"

The other cops rubbed bleary eyes and shrugged. "Sure, why not?" one of them replied apathetically.

"Nine coffees — and make it snappy!" He turned to me and asked casually, "You want one too, Bert?"

"Why not? Might as well celebrate."

"Okay, make that ten," he ordered before the uniformed policeman had left the room. Next, the inspector went behind the desk to pick up the phone and called M ——, his boss.

"He won't listen to any deals. We're calling it a day, if that's okay with you. We're all exhausted — that is, all of us except him. He's fresh as a daisy."

". . . ?"

"Of course we tried that. For the time being, you won't get anything out of him. He wants to see his lawyer first. Then he'll probably decide to talk."

". . . ?"

"We'll let him get a few hours' sleep, then see that he shaves. He's got to look good for the press; otherwise they'll be accusing us of brutality on top of everything else."

". . ."

"All right. Good night, monsieur."

And wham! that coffee hit me.

We talked while sipping our coffee. A real friendly conversation. Why not? We were old pals by then. Mainly, the conversation centered on the heist — its spectacular side, the accounts in the papers, some funny anecdotes.

Meanwhile, like an idiot, I was getting higher and higher. God, was I happy! Just bursting with pride — and Benzedrine. Those bastards had slipped me a Mickey in the coffee. They'd managed to put one over on me.

I was trembling with overexcitement and happiness. "What the hell! Why shouldn't I tell you?" And that thing I use for a brain revved itself up. Oh, what a delicious drunk! My hands shook, but this in no way prevented me from swaggering. I was watching myself, admiring myself in their eyes. A little more, and I'd have done the dance of the seven veils.

My brain started whirring like a computer, clicking away as I fed and sorted information, then analyzed it. The detectives stood there in open-mouthed amazement.

"Give me a cigarette, please. How about a light? Thanks. All right, let's get one thing straight. I'm not going to do any more

talking until you bring me to a high government official, somebody who's willing to live up to the terms of our 'contract.' On
the other hand, let me make this clear right now: I will supply
details concerning only my own involvement in this heist. You
just won't be getting names from me. Not even if you slip me
a whole bottle of Benzedrine!"

Benzedrine, that's fuel for the feeble-minded, the impotent.
The cheap wine they gave French soldiers before attacks in
World War I, that was nothing. Put Benzedrine in your motor,
and you're really spaced-out. They could have handed me fifty
years for congenital idiocy, and I would have done the sentence
standing on my head.

But names — never!

No hard feelings, Sherlock. Even with the screwing, the experience was worthwhile.

Drugs are here to stay. Jesus Christ, we could have used the
stuff in Indo-China. It was enough to make you cry, and I didn't
want to make myself any more idiotic than I was already
— but it felt so good, releasing all those taut springs inside my
brain. It felt good, shining like a star and — somehow —
winning.

You've got to make the most of it; nobody stays in the
limelight very long. I've seen dozens of escapes. Somehow the
wind-up was always like a bad hangover.

In a few hours, when I woke up, I'd have my back to the wall
again. It was either do or die. Some people have come, seen, and
conquered. Me, I talked, signed, and woke up.

And there I was — alone again. All on my own as usual,
dangling from my chute, dangling from my destiny.

CHAPTER 26

It's All a Big Joke

"IT'S ALL A BIG JOKE." In the old days, convicts had this motto tattooed across their foreheads. Me, I've got it tattooed across my soul.

Good morning, prison.

It takes you a long time to get over the sourish smell of that soup. At first, it's something you just tolerate; after a while, it gets to be home.

We said good-bye rather sadly, the detectives and I, for we'd become friends. That's the way it always was. In thirty years of traveling, this was my twenty-third jail.

I was welcomed back by Police Sergeant Ben Guigui. "Oh, bravo, Monsieur Spaggiari!" He opened his big ledger. Last name, first and middle names, date of birth, previous convictions, religion, last year of school completed. He never stopped laughing as he wrote.

"But why the devil did you confess?"

"Why not? It was more fun that way."

"More fun! Well, you'll see that things are nice and quiet around here. And actually, it isn't all that bad. Things have changed a lot since the time . . ."

Keep talking, you big ape. I've been hearing that same old

refrain for thirty years. Nothing ever changes in prison. No, I take that back. The screws had grown older and seemed to have lost their taste for corporal punishment. Unfortunately, they'd lost their taste for corruption as well. That had sent prices skyrocketing. Clandestine mail was exorbitant, and the whiskey must have been flown over direct from Scotland.

Yes, I guess Ben Guigui was right; things had changed. In the old days you could order meals from outside, and there was coffee at the canteen. Nowadays, nothing doing. And then, there used to be wire-mesh screens in the visiting room. You could hear yourself without screaming; you could even feel the breath of someone you loved. Now, with that damned Hygia-phone, the person's face looked all blurred.

On the other hand, there was the radio and TV on Sunday afternoons for those who'd behaved and done their work properly. But there wasn't any TV for prisoners awaiting trial. Nor could you play cards like in the old days.

Well, that was it. Back in jail. Ben Guigui shook my hand and turned me over to the supply-room guard. He, too, gave me a friendly handshake. "Monsieur Spaggiari, in all my thirty years of service, I've never seen anything as fine as that."

Afterward, they searched me. They no longer poke around in your anus nowadays — they just make you cough. Once I'd complied with this formality, they brought me to the division sergeant. This guy was stiff and businesslike.

"Don't vorry, here you get goot treatment," he said with a thick Alsatian accent. I'd just been searched, but the son of a bitch shook me down again. "Rules are rules. Shtrip und make it shnappy. Don't try to get zo shmart. Come, *schnell.* Bend forvart — all de vay ofer! So, now you get dressed. Don't let my accent gif you de idea dot I'm a fool. I taught myself French. I read all de papers."

Christ, I felt like I was back in the Middle Ages. The way the bars rang out against the vaulted ceiling, the footsteps echoing over and over. You take whatever those walls give you — it's all yours. In a few seconds you're right back in the swing of things. You're thirty years lighter and thirty years heavier. You wanted to conquer the world, but, instead, a narrow door opens. It's the cell for newcomers.

"Welcome aboard, Bert." The guard gives you a big smile because he's glad to see you. Then the door clangs shut. Suddenly, you're all alone again. All alone with those old wounds that remind you of rough times. When you're in a mess like that, the years don't matter much anymore. You realize that you've always lived one dream too late; a drink, a morning, a night, a train, or a sweetheart too late. In prison, everything goes through your mind. You've got to watch out for that.

A little later that day, they put a young Algerian in with me. I would rather have been by myself. The first day you prefer being alone; afterward, everything changes. I don't recall why he'd been sent up. I only remember that he was a Kabyle. He reminded me of another Berber tribesman — Ali, the son of a chieftain, a barbarian who'd received a battlefield promotion to sergeant. Not many Algerians made sergeant at twenty.

That was back in Indo-China at the beginning of '54. Ali Mérina came in from the field one afternoon and, as he could no longer enter the canteen for corporals, headed for the NCO mess. As luck would have it, he ran into a bunch of guys who were already drunk. "No wogs in here!" they told him.

He didn't give a damn about their insults. He just wanted a drink. So bad that he'd come straight from the field without changing out of battle dress. He walked right up to the bar. Five or six NCOs piled on him and sent him flying out into the company street. Ali fought back, and, as luck would have it, the loaded submachine gun slung over his shoulder went off, killing one man.

It had been an accident. An unfortunate one, but an accident nonetheless. I'd seen worse than that in the battalion, and they'd always hushed it up. Our sergeant major got the gate, and the young officer who took his place refused to settle things out of court. Ali Mérina wound up in front of a general court-martial.

Those were bad times. A period when France used her soldiers' hides to wipe away her own humiliations.

I was with him the day he went before the court-martial. The president looked unnaturally pale. On his list appeared the name Ali Mérina, and yet they had brought him a white man. (Ali was blond and blue-eyed, which isn't uncommon for a Kabyle.)

"What are you — an Arab?"

Wham! Better not call a Kabyle an Arab . . .

"I'm no goddamned Arab. I'm a Kabyle, god damn you!"

Bam! Sentenced to death.

Nobody in the stockade believed the news, the guards any more than prisoners. I told myself that if a guy didn't have the right to curse a judge, then they were bound to give me the death sentence. At the time, that wouldn't have bothered me.

In those days, the system of military justice was plain madness. For instance, a guy could get twenty years at hard labor for rape without the use of force. Meanwhile, there was no such thing as rape in the Vietnamese criminal code. By tradition, women just let themselves be raped, then received a settlement — two weeks' pay, which the army withheld from the "rapist."

At any rate, Ali Mérina went back to his cell to await execution. But he kept hoping for a reprieve. With a French premier like Vincent Auriol, he had another think coming.

Sentenced to hard labor, I occupied the cell next door. One day Ali struck a guard who was beating another prisoner. Two weeks in solitary. When they brought him back up, the warden said he'd obtained a reprieve, that he could take it easy. Everything would be all right once he got back to France.

Hanoi. Barracks Number 32. May, June, July, August 1954. Forty of us jammed into one small room. The only window measured eighteen inches by twelve inches. Meanwhile, in the mess-watchtower located upstairs, lawyers, judges, provost marshals, and wardens threw wild parties with their Vietnamese girl friends and their white whores. While they danced and drank, we were dying on the floor below. And even with all their orgies, they managed to line their pockets. There were plenty of illicit deals, opportunities on the black market. For instance, they would buy collections of jade and lock them up in the vault of the Société Générale.

November 1954. The ship. Soon we'd be in France.

I shudder with hate and disgust, thinking of all those days, those chains — and of my own stupidity.

We stopped in Suez. We offered to take up a collection for Ali Mérina so that he could escape. But the idiot refused. He felt sure he'd win a reprieve. He wanted to go home to his father with honor.

December 1954. France! I'd made it back to my own country and, thank God, I was still alive.

There was a band on the pier; we could hear them playing from our sealed compartment below the waterline. We could somehow sense that the sky was blue. We waited for hours. Suddenly, policemen appeared. Lots of policemen. They shackled us together by the ankles and wrists.

"For God's sake! You don't mean it! You can't be holding us! The damned war is over. This is France! Jesus, we've been in the front lines and fought like good soldiers. We're back in our own country, damn it! We didn't do anything!"

Hours later, when there wasn't a soul on the pier, they rigged a gangway for us. The convicts debarked. The skies over France were gray. Our wretched column moved off, our chains rattling against the cobblestones.

February 1955. The Baumettes prison in Marseille.

That evening, Bouculat, the barber, was cutting Ali Mérina's hair. "Say, you've still got your Indo-China bonus coming. You can really have a ball if you want to."

"No, I'm saving my money to buy some decent clothes. I want to look right when I get out."

The following night, a guard woke Campocasso, the janitor. He told him to start spreading blankets over the floor in the corridor.*

"Jesus! Who's getting it?"

"Mérina."

"*No!* That can't be!"

"It's true — they're going to execute him."

A dozen guards had massed in front of Ali's cell.

Noiselessly, one of them inserted the key into the lock, then waited. At a signal, they all went pouring inside and pinned him down to his mat. Ali Mérina struggled fiercely, then he realized . . .

The warden walked up to him. "Be brave; your plea has been rejected."

"Okay. You can let me up. It's all right."

They didn't need to drag him in the corridors; no ritual with the shirt collar either. He wasn't going to the guillotine — he was a trooper, so he'd face the firing squad. Before leaving

---

*Blankets are spread over the floor so that the condemned man's feet won't be harmed when he struggles with guards.

the corridor, Ali said good-by to Campocasso. Then they led him to Fort Saint-Nicolas. It was 5:00 A.M. The firing squad didn't turn up until half an hour later. For thirty minutes, Ali Mérina and the warden paced up and down. Ali was barefoot.

"You caught me off guard. I don't even know what I'm supposed to think or what I should say now that I'm about to die."

The warden's face went white as a sheet. It was the warden who told this story to P —— , who'd been serving as a dentist for the Baumettes prison at the time. The warden called it the most painful experience in his life.

I'm not out to reform the world. It is what it is. I've never been corrupt enough to face the world with luck on my side. That's why guys like Mérina or me can never survive.

The next day, I was taken out of the newcomers' cell. I had to be kept in solitary, so they moved me to the maximum-security block. My cell was clean, the floor tiled, and, prize of all prizes, it had its own toilet bowl and washstand.

A prisoner from Bordeaux got somebody to pass me instant coffee and sugar. Dédé got me books and newspapers. Lule managed to slip me a stove made of two tin cans.

The guards took turns coming to see the "wonder" in his cell. Some even let themselves in to congratulate me and chat for a while. Others simply hid behind the peephole. In the old days, convicts would amuse themselves by poking the guards' eyes out with thin metal pens. Nowadays, this kind of fun isn't possible because they've put glass over the peepholes. And then, most guards wear rubber-soled sandals, so you can't even hear them coming. Some prisoners do manage to tame mice that warn them of the guards' coming. Those little suckers work more efficiently than any radar set.

Guy came to see me. He'd made lieutenant. In Indo-China and Algeria, he'd been a hero. His last wound, resulting from a burst of machine-gun fire, practically cut him in two. For this, he was entitled to a good pension and a privileged (!) position. But he'd visited me without authorization, so he drew a reprimand and a final warning. It seems that the guard who threw him out had himself taken part in the riots of 1968.

The roster of guards in my cell block included Galinette, Tarzan, Hitler (there's always a Hitler somewhere), Bab el Oued, and, last but not least, Sèlou. Wrongly suspected of giving a lawyer's name to one of the prisoners, Sèlou was transferred to another division.

Jealousy, infighting, distrust, personal ambition, schizophrenia — it's the same rat race as on the outside. The only difference is that prisons tend to be small, so you see things more clearly. And as it's all crowded into one place, the rottenness stinks even worse.

I'm used to doing time. I can tell you that jails don't have much effect on human nature. But experience had taught me that the world wasn't so clean outside those walls, either. Sure, Nice looks great when you see it as a tourist, stopping at the Hôtel Négresco for a few days and strolling along the Promenade des Anglais, steering a sailboat over the Bay of Angels.

But I mean the inside story. I know enough about the Riviera's seamy side to make your hair stand on end. The immorality and vice would supply me with material for several books.

Just take a nice quiet little town like Hyères, for example. It's one of the most charming spots you could imagine. It looks like it hasn't changed since the time of Queen Victoria, with its cool alleys, its red-tiled rooftops, its gardens, its pine forests right at the edge of the Mediterranean. Perhaps the most beautiful town in Europe. I know Hyères very well, having spent my childhood and a good part of my life there.

It was when I returned from those five years at hard labor to which I'd been sentenced by the Hanoi court-martial. I came back to Hyères because I had no other choice. I'd been banished from Nice for twenty years. Which meant that for twenty years I was forbidden to set foot in that city or any other place on the French border. In addition, I had to have my ticket punched each month by the law enforcement agency nearest my domicile.

I tried to live that way. Maybe it doesn't sound bad, but actually it's impossible. If the police happen to stop you during a routine road check, it means spending a whole day at the police station. Nine times out of ten, they rough you up. Or else you just go limp and let them insult you. In town, it's worse. Anybody who wants to retain even a shred of his dignity has to go into hiding. Otherwise, you're going to take it on the chin or knuckle under and become a police informer.

Yet I was awfully happy to get back to France. I was dazzled by the sunlight; I gazed at the most ordinary things as though they were miracles of human ingenuity and good taste.

CHAPTER 27

He'll Be Here, He Won't Be Here

I WAS STILL WAITING for a friend. I'd been in jail four months and twelve days, and every Wednesday night I went through that same anguish: he'll be here, he won't be here. Now, I couldn't take it anymore. I was fed up, fed up to the teeth.

In fact, I believe it was that day, Wednesday, March 9, 1977, when I got to the root of this business. For sixteen Thursdays, not counting the ones when I didn't go there, I'd been leaving the prison at 2:00 P.M. and going to the court building. That would have been ample time for him to get ready and make up his mind. There was no point in doing any more daydreaming — it simply meant that I'd had it. He wasn't going to come now.

I was forty-four years old, and, despite the fact that they had no evidence against me (except my own statement, which was nothing conclusive), I would be getting a fifteen-to twenty-year sentence.

Fifteen to twenty years! No, messieurs, I've been through all that. I don't have the slightest interest in doing it again. I'd stalled for time, stretching out my preliminary investigation as long as I could; now the deadline was approaching. I was ready to meet my fate.

I'd been training myself mentally. I knew that I could open the window of your chamber and jump, in the twinkling of an eye. Maybe I'd be doing it the next day or, at the latest, on the following Thursday.

I knew that my friend wouldn't be coming now. He won't come, he won't come, I kept telling myself. You've got to get that idea out of your head. I hoped that, of all those cops, there'd be one who could shoot straighter than the rest. I already knew the spot where I'd fall — on the pedestrian crosswalk across from the Le Pastrouil restaurant, belonging to my friend Henri. "Anarchists always die on pedestrian crosswalks." I wanted to have enough time to shout "Death to the goddamned cops!" I also hoped there'd be some charitable person to lend me a gun so that the police wouldn't take me alive. But even without this kind individual, I'd kill myself somehow before falling back into their hands.

I've never asked anything of you, God, so give me what you please. Give me whatever you can! I'll be ready. Amen.

Whether they ended in freedom or death, my plans had been laid with the utmost care. During the first hearings in the judge's chamber, my handcuffs had been removed, but the two guards remained with us. Somehow, as those Thursday afternoon cross-examinations went on week after week, I sensed mutual trust growing between the judge and myself. So much so that, one afternoon, he asked the guards to wait in the room next door. There was nothing so strange about the request — I didn't have a reputation for being dangerous. What's more, he would have had to get them to leave one way or another, because my dossier held certain data of a political nature that could not be made known.

The place was a small, overheated room. There were four of us inside: my lawyer, Maître Jacques Peyrat; Judge Richard Bouazis; the court clerk, Mme. Hoareau; and myself. The hearings began at 3:00 P.M. and, as a rule, lasted until 4:00.

The judge's desk separated me from the window. I therefore had to find a way of going around it. As a matter of fact, I'd already done just that when explaining one technicality or other about the maps that I was drawing for him. Yet every time I'd gone too close to the window, he'd become uneasy. I had to allow for this. For the day of my jump, I'd prepared a map of the sewers — this subject really fascinated him. And I'd drawn it on three sheets of paper that had to be placed edge to edge. So it stood to reason that he'd have to ask me to arrange them for him. And that would be just what the doctor ordered. I'd go up and lean over his shoulder. This would put me within four or five feet of the window.

It was one that overlooked the rue de la Préfecture. The sidewalk waited for me twenty-four feet below.

The friend who should have come for me knew all this. The newspapers had written exhaustively about the case. Everybody knew that Judge Bouazis would be examining the case. It was easy enough to learn the location of his chamber.

Okay, I told myself, harping on this won't do you any good.

Now that there was no choice, I had to straighten out my affairs. I drew up a letter for Audi, another for my mother. I didn't intend to mail them; instead, I'd keep them with me in case that lunatic actually did come to get me the next day. Meanwhile, I had to keep those letters hidden — *but good.* They could wreck my whole plan. I had a trick for keeping the letters from being discovered, even if the cops searched me carefully. Without this little secret, I'd never have risked writing them.

The Wednesday night inspections were pretty rough. One by one they searched thoroughly all books and newspapers in your cell; they poked around in corners, felt under everything. They were experts — but so was I.

The supper pail came. The evening went by. Prison routine never varies.

Yet it still wasn't so bad there in detention, awaiting my trial. It wasn't like being in stir. You got to see your lawyer; you went before the examining judge. You still hadn't lost all touch with the outside, with life.

That's why I'd sworn never to go back into stir. I'd die first. You don't know what it's like to do time. I can't explain it to you. I can only tell you it's worse than my suicidal plan. I'd probably be called a coward. Frankly, I didn't give a damn what people thought. I'd been a dead man since drinking that coffee à la Benzedrine. Sure, I laughed with the guards, put on the cry act with Bouazis, and pretended to Peyrat to be interested in my defense. But that didn't change a damned thing.

Four months is enough for your instincts and thoughts to settle. It doesn't take long for a poet to turn into a bookkeeper in jail.

And then night came. The weight of my thoughts — some vital, others trifling — grew oppressive, pulling me down into a deep sleep.

You wake up in prison with the clang of steel gratings, the rattle of locks, the bawling of the day's first orders: roll call, cleanup, coffee. But Thursday morning was also shower day, which suited me fine. Like that, I'd always be nice and clean when I went to see the judge.

I hadn't been taken to see him on the previous Thursday. It was the first time I'd ever missed. I found it odd, and hoped that nothing had changed. Going to the laundry room, I button-holed Riquier, a guard only months from retirement. He assured me that they'd be coming at 2:00 P.M. to escort me to the courthouse.

That was all I needed to hear. I was happy. I'd stay happy right up to the end.

Eleven-thirty: lunch pail. I ate. I felt great. In fact, I was amazed at how good I felt. Then I went to the window while waiting for the guards to come. A beautiful Rhone Valley sky stretched into infinity. Not far away, the workmen renovating the prison were having a snack. From time to time, I would say hello or try to get a rise out of one of them. If it was a French-man, he'd either tell me to go fuck myself or pretend he hadn't heard. On the other hand, if it was an Arab, he'd always reply with a friendly wave or with a smile.

Around 1:30 P.M., the warden walked by underneath my window and gave me a big wave. I immediately saw that as a good omen. Furthermore, my horoscope was great for that day. It looked like I could get away with most anything. Time would tell.

Two o'clock on the dot. Footsteps echoed in the corridor. They approached my cell, then, all at once, died out at my door. The key buried itself in the lock. The bolt shot back. The heavy steel door swung open.

"Spaggiari — courthouse!"

"Present!"

I shook scores of hands as I walked through the prison. That's the way it was each time out. Everybody wanted to touch me for luck.

A few minutes later, they handcuffed me and helped me into

the back of the paddy wagon. I knew none of the men inside.
And they all looked too worried for any conversation. Then
what gets into the van with us but a girl! Jesus Christ, she was
a prisoner, too. And a real looker. A half-caste who could
knock your eye out. We kept on staring throughout the whole
trip, fidgeting on our seats and panting like madmen. Not more
than three feet separated me from that doll. If only a plane
could have bombed the city just then.

Christ, if I didn't stop staring at her, I'd go fuckin' crazy. I
looked out the little rear window. We'd just turned down the
boulevard Jean-Jaurès. It was a fine day. Not so long before, I'd
been watching anxiously whenever I visited the courthouse.
It had been arranged with my friend that on D-Day he
was to attract my attention as he drove past the paddy wagon
at some point on our route. Yes, that's what had been
arranged.

In a few moments, Jacques Peyrat would be waiting for me
on the courthouse steps, as he did every Thursday. He'd served
in Indo-China and Algeria. I represented a big case for him: his
photos splashed in the papers, interviews on TV. He put everything he had into my defense. He tried to make me out to be
some kind of poor orphan when, actually, I had no excuse. My
conscience didn't bother me in the least. Lawyers are great for
hoods and chumps. You need to be wearing battle dress to
defend me.

The driver jammed his foot on the brake at the red light and,
as if by accident, we all fell against the girl, even the guys sitting
in front of her. I took the opportunity to ask her for the right
time, as she was the only one whose watch hadn't been confi-
scated.

"Two-twenty-five," she replied, in a sultry voice. It was a bit
husky, exciting. The men began sweating heavily. Well, it was

rather warm inside there. I turned my head absently. On the right, a big motorcycle had slid between the paddy wagon and the curb. It was one of those really sophisticated machines. Under the heavy helmet, the motorcyclist's eyes met mine — and instantly I froze.

The light turned green, and, amid an infernal racket, the powerful machine went racing away.

That wasn't any "friend." That was Biki, my Tuareg man.

CHAPTER 28

Spaggiari Has Flown the Coop!

My heart was beating wildly and I had electricity in my fingertips. Was it really on for today? Had he attracted my attention for *that?* I went on sweating it out until the paddy wagon slowed down at the end of the rue du Marché, just before crossing the rue de la Préfecture, where it would turn. When we got there, I glanced to my left. Scaffolding had been erected outside the courthouse, just beyond the judge's window. Biki had parked his motorcycle at the foot of that scaffolding.

Squatting beside the machine, with his helmet still on, he was busy polishing the chrome-plated rim of his front wheel.

During the two or three seconds that our driver spent making the turn, Biki held up one hand, spreading all five fingers. That could mean only one thing: at 5:00 P.M., I was to climb out onto the judge's window ledge and jump.

Now the paddy wagon came to a stop in the courtyard of the big building. In climbing out, my hand grazed the girl's arm. She looked at me, smiling imperceptibly. Only a shy smile, but it meant she'd seen that luck was running my way. We'd soon find out.

Two guards assigned to the court building took charge of me and led me straight to the judge's chamber.

As usual, Maître Peyrat was waiting for me at the top of the marble stairway. "How's everything, Bert?" he asked, squeezing my manacled hands between his palms. "Say, you look awfully drawn. You aren't coming down with something, are you, Bert?"

"I've got a damned toothache that's killing me."

The two cops gave me a little breather, so the lawyer and I went and sat down on the bench in the corridor. He started off right away with: "Here's your cigars, Bert. Here, let me give you a light." I was puffing away on one of the stogies while he straightened his black robe.

"Today, I think the judge is going to question you about the way you came out of the Paillon. Bert, I think you ought to . . ."

The court clerk, Mme. Hoareau, had just stuck her head out the door. "Judge Bouazis is ready to see you now."

First, we went into her office, where the guards removed my handcuffs. Then I entered the judge's chamber, followed by my lawyer.

"Good afternoon, Your Honor."

The judge was seated behind his desk. He waved us to two empty chairs. Somehow, he looked more like a doctor than a judge. About thirty-five or forty, Jewish-looking, kind of short, with a big lock of black hair that almost covered one of his thick lenses.

His eyes, prying but conciliatory, ran over me like greedy insects. "You look a bit on the pale side today, Spaggiari."

"Well, you know, it's sort of shady where I am . . ."

"He's got a toothache, Your Honor."

"Oh, that's too bad."

I was trying hard not to look at the window. That could have given the whole thing away. But somehow that window kept crowding into my eyes.

"Hey, there! I've just asked you if you're up to answering questions today."

"Oh, excuse me, judge. Yes, yes, I'll be fine."

Satisfied, he consulted the two sheets of paper that he'd just removed from my thick file. Meanwhile, Mme. Hoareau smiled at me as she returned to her seat at the typewriter.

The judge cleared his throat. "Yes, your story has a great many points that don't . . . But we're just going to drop all that for the time being!" he decided, flattening his hand over the two sheets of paper. This move raised the sleeve of his robe slightly, and I could see the dial on his watch. It was 3:20 P.M.

"The last time you came before me, two weeks ago, we had to stop at the point where you left the vault with your loot. I'd like you to explain just how you did that."

"Well, Your Honor, each guy grabbed a suitcase, and we just got the hell out of there."

"How many suitcases were there?"

"Now, that I don't remember."

"And yet you'd split up the loot. It's impossible for you not to remember!"

"Well, the only thing I have to go by is that there were forty of us and we each carried one of them."

"Yes, and I suppose your name is Ali Baba. Okay. Very funny. Listen, Spaggiari, we know the approximate amount of cash and negotiable papers you took from the bank. [You're just kidding yourself, judge, if you think all those box-holders told you the truth! More than a few of them would rather keep mum about their losses than answer your questions.] But the point isn't crucial and I doubt that this detail could alter anything in your system of defense."

He was one shrewd customer, that Bouazis. A little detail here, a little detail there, until he had a regular billy club in his hands. Talk about clubs, I still hadn't forgotten (or forgiven) the trick he'd pulled at our previous hearing, two weeks before. My wife had just been grilled for forty-eight hours straight, and Bouazis had threatened to have her indicted for aiding and abetting. Hell, that's what I call taking hostages!

"My client can no longer remember this technicality. And it's quite understandable. There were a lot of them, and some of the suitcases must have been full, others half-full, others almost empty."

Ataboy, defend your investment. Those are the last few plays you're going to run in this ballgame. One way or another, you're losing your biggest client in the next few minutes.

The suitcases, the rain, the flashlights, the brand of batteries we used, footprints . . . Time was going by. And the more it went by, the more feverish I became.

The last time I'd caught sight of the judge's wrist watch, it showed 4:05. How long ago had that been? Forty minutes ago, fifty minutes ago, an hour ago? I was completely confused! Was it time to pull out my map of the sewers? I'd have only that one chance to go behind his desk. Only one. If I muffed it, I was screwed.

As for asking them the time, nothing could have seemed more suspicious, unless, maybe, asking for a goddamned ladder. Oh, shit, I was going to fuck up, but good. I felt it coming.

Mme. Hoareau's arms were bare, but her watch was much too small. Besides, her wrists never stopped jumping around over her typewriter.

Then an idea came to me. "The suitcases were made of aluminum. The brand was Alcañir!"

"Well, well." Bouazis beamed, his posterior jiggling on the chair.

"Could you spell that name?" asked Mme. Hoareau.

"Well, I think . . . No, I remember. A-L-K-I . . . No, it's A-L-C . . . Ha! Ha! I'll have to see it written to be able to spell it."

I got up to go over to her, but I'd barely unstuck myself from the chair when the judge practically shouted, "Remain seated!" and handed me a pad and a ballpoint.

Oh, shit! What was eating that guy? I'd never seen him so wary before. That looked bad, damn it!

I started sweating. And my fingers shook when I wrote "Alcañir" on the pad. I held it out to Mme. Hoareau so that she'd come over to get it. She got to her feet unhesitatingly. Only, as soon as she left her chair, I drew my hand back, to force her to come right up to my chair.

"See, there's a tilde over the *n.*"

She leaned over my left side, practically touching me. Oh, Christ, she kept both hands behind her back!

"What is a tilde?"

"It's like this — look." I made a kind of an *s* sideways over the *n.* "That's Spanish. It means you've got to pronounce it like *nyi.* That makes Alca*nyir.*"

Then I handed her the pad. Her watch was on her right wrist, and she reached for the pad with her left hand. I pretended to lose my grip on the pad, letting it fall onto the carpet. Immediately, she stooped to pick it up — once more with her left hand! She kept her other arm behind her back, like a goddamned figure skater. Oh, Jesus! I'd never seen anything like it! I thought I'd go out of my mind. I had to be on that goddamned window ledge at five fuckin' o'clock! The whole operation had to go off in a few seconds, and I didn't even know what fuckin' time it was! I wasn't even ready. I lunged out to get the pad ahead of her. In so doing, I jostled her. The judge and the lawyer both got to their feet. God only knows what they imagined.

"Here you are, madame. I'm very sorry. Awfully clumsy of me."

And she took the pad from me with both hands. Her watch showed 4:58.

I sagged back into my chair. Instantly, my hand plunged into my pocket to unearth the map of the sewers.

"I've got something here that may interest you, Your Honor," I stammered weakly, offering him the three sheets of paper.

Just as he took them, the phone rang. Mme. Hoareau picked up the receiver and spoke; meanwhile, the judge unfolded the maps I'd just given him.

"Oh, it's the sewers! Very interesting. But there's just one thing . . ."

"Monsieur Bouazis, excuse me. It's for you."

"Very good. Just switch it to my line, will you? Hello? Yes, of course! Where are you? Certainly; I'm coming right down."

He hung up and got to his feet. "I'm going to step outside for a few minutes." He opened the door and asked the two guards to keep an eye on me while he was away.

Somebody revved up the engine of a big motorcycle just under the window. Trouble was, one of the cops stood right in front of it; the other guarded the door.

"What's the matter? You really look pale. Do you want me to . . . ?" inquired Maître Peyrat.

"Forget it!" I interrupted angrily. "I'll feel better in a moment."

"Here, take my handkerchief. Wipe your face."

"No, I've got my own."

Mme. Hoareau was looking at me compassionately.

"I know what it's like having a toothache."

Downstairs, the motorcycle was still making a racket.

Peyrat handed me a cigar. I lit it. Greedily, I sucked the smoke into my lungs.

If it isn't on for today, it'll be on for next Thursday, I told myself. Biki won't let me down now that he's here in Nice.

"How much longer do I have to keep coming to see the judge?" I asked, fighting the urge to spring out of the chair.

"Just one or two more sessions, now. After that, everything will be fine. Don't worry. But while we're on the subject, I think that the judge is planning to go down into the sewers with you next Thursday."

"Then we don't meet here?"

"No, we'll meet at the Palais des Expositions. Don't worry, I'll be there to help you."

That's what he thought! If I wasn't coming to the court building on the following Thursday, then it wouldn't work that week, either. There was no way of letting Biki know. I didn't even know where he lived.

Now he was really feeding gas, racing the motor.

The door of the other office swung shut. It was the judge. He came back into the chamber a few seconds later.

"Now, where were we?"

Right away, the two cops slipped out, closing the door behind them.

Bouazis mopped his brow in front of the window. "Madame

Hoareau, would you kindly turn off the steam? I'm roasting in here."

Finally, he made up his mind and returned to the desk. "Now, where were we again? Ah, yes, the sewers — they interest me enormously," he remarked, as if talking to himself. Then he pushed aside my maps, saying, "I'll take a look at them tomorrow morning. Right now, it's five-o-five, so let's wind up with your statement for today. Read back the last line, Madame Hoareau."

Electricity surged through my body. I still had a chance. It was now or never!

Before the woman could utter a word, I broke in. "Your Honor, there are some technical details about the map that you may not understand. It's made in three parts."

"Oh, so you want to clarify certain points, eh?"

"I drew that map on the basis of firsthand experience with the places involved. A few things might not be too clear to anyone else. You know how it is."

He picked up the three sheets. Then he spread them carefully on his desk.

"For once, you're being cooperative. I don't want to pass up this opportunity."

The racket of the motorcycle died out abruptly.

"Well, which way is this sheet supposed to go?"

"Want me to show you?"

"Go right ahead. You aren't exactly a genius when it comes to drawing. I'm convinced that a psychiatrist would be able to read a great deal about your character from this."

I rose from my chair. Before going around his desk, I casually snuffed out the stump of my cigar in the ashtray.

My brain was still working at lightning speed. Open the window. Swing my leg over the sill; I was okay in that department. I felt sure nobody in the world could move faster than I could. Just one trouble: after I got past the ledge, there was that twenty-four-foot drop. I wasn't exactly a kid anymore, and nine chances out of ten I'd break both legs. And what about Biki? Was he still down there?

Should I jump or shouldn't I? I didn't know what to do. This wasn't just some attempt at escape — I knew that. This was all or nothing. I was going for broke. I made up my mind. I'd jump, no matter what.

Slowly, I walked around the desk. I went right by the window without hesitating. And then I was standing over the judge's shoulder. At once, I put the three sheets in order. Next, I picked up a red pencil and marked all the junctions. Sweat was pouring off me; my hands shook; my breathing was far too rapid, far too shallow. The judge would sense something and start screaming his head off. God almighty, I had to say something!

Fortunately, my voice came out calm. "I'm sorry, but I'm not feeling well. Something's wrong with these teeth of mine. Do you see this? It's the Palais des Expositions. And this here, that's the manhole we started using back in . . ."

I kept feeding him details. I knew he'd always been uncomfortable whenever I got too close to the window. Now he was beginning to lose himself in thought.

"What about the little island — where's that?"

"Here, where the cross is. And see this here? That's the culvert leading into the Chauvain main sewer."

"Now that you show me these things, it all looks clear. Fine. I'll study it tomorrow morning."

"Okay."

I'd just heaved a weary sigh as he began folding the three sheets before placing them in a folder. I pivoted slowly and headed back to my chair. As I reached the corner of his desk,

I sprang to the window, flipped the bolt, threw open the French window with one motion, swung my leg over the sill. At once, the engine of a powerful motorcycle kicked up a racket. It took only a split second to plan my fall.

"No, not that!" screamed Peyrat behind me.

Stand up, hook up — Go! I leaped out in space. First, I rebounded off the narrow ledge over the building's main doorway; from there, I took a long jump onto the roof of a Renault 6; then down into the street. As I landed, my glasses popped out of my pocket. My first impulse was to pick them up. But I resisted the urge. The judge was already at the window, screaming at the top of his lungs, *"Stop thief! Stop him, somebody!"*

The big machine was there beside me. I straddled it and thumbed my nose at Bouazis and Peyrat in the window. Then I wrapped my arms around Biki's quilted body armor and VROOOM!

The whole thing hadn't taken more than eight seconds.

A moment later, the motorcycle went roaring into the basement garage of an apartment building, while four thousand cops, gendarmes, and CRS were mobilized for all-out war. Me, I was transferred to a British limousine, or, to be more precise, I dove through a trap door into a hiding place under the back seat. And the limousine slid out of the garage at a stately five miles an hour. We drove across town and went through the roadblocks, fourteen of them between Nice and Paris. They even made the driver open the trunk at the toll booth outside Aix-en-Provence.

My hostess kept stuffing me with sandwiches and whiskey, passed through a smaller trap door under the elbow rest.

We had the radio going all night. I was sure that my pals in prison were clinking their lunch pails against the bars every time a news flash informed them that Spaggiari had managed to get through the enemy lines.

Everyone in France must have been laughing their heads off. There's your story.

Like my grandfather and his father before him, I must abandon my wife, my dogs, my herds, and my rifles.

Farewell, native land. I'll be back in twenty years or twenty centuries. I'm free.

—Completed, late 1977, on the hidden side of the moon

Postscript

In 1978, *Paris-Match,* the leading French journalistic maga-
zine, assigned Arnaud Hamelin and Hubert Lassier to the job
of tracking down Albert Spaggiari and getting an interview
with him. It turned out to be as complicated and suspenseful
as something in a John Le Carré novel. First, they discovered
a woman who had known Spaggiari in Nice, and she put them
in touch with Catena, a network made up of soldiers of fortune
from many countries — former foreign legionnaires, ex –
HOAS men, Greeks who had supported the colonels' regime,
Portuguese partisans of Salazar, and others.

The trail led to Spain, where an attractive Spanish woman,
representing Catena, directed the reporters to a rendezvous
with a bearded man in the lobby of the Plaza Hotel in Madrid.
He was a tall, rangy man with hair so long that it seemed to
be a wig and a beard that was obviously fake — it kept slipping.
When Hamelin and Lassier began to speak with him, they
heard a lilt of the Riviera accent in his speech and a hearty
laugh. This was Albert Spaggiari in his joking disguise.

They took a walk through the Madrid streets, Spaggiari playing with his false beard and mustache and, from time to time,
removing them. Spaggiari explained that he had undergone

plastic surgery in Brazil. "I needed a face lift, anyway," he explained, "and it makes me look ten years younger. I'm having fun," he added.

The three men arrived at the Club 31, one of Madrid's most elegant restaurants. There was a difficult moment — Spaggiari was not wearing a jacket. A gentleman does not lunch at Club 31 unless he is in proper attire, the headwaiter explained. Somebody went off and procured a kind of zoot-suit jacket, a relic of the forties, and a tie about three inches too wide.

When they had sat down and ordered, Spaggiari remarked, "There's nothing worse than working on an empty stomach." At that, his mustache came unstuck on one side, so he peeled it off for good. "There were sixty million francs in that vault," he went on. "It was like being in Ali Baba's cave — but you know what? Once we got inside, our first idea was to have a good feed. We had plenty of wine and food down there, so we ate and drank for over an hour with all those lovely safe-deposit boxes staring us in the face."

But what about his escape? The reporters were eager to hear about that.

Spaggiari smiled and talked a little about Richard Bouazis, the judge through whose chamber window he had jumped. He had liked Bouazis, he said. "I feel kind of guilty about fooling him with that map routine."

What happened after the jump from the window? Things grew a little vaguer here. Spaggiari, hidden in the limousine, had reached Paris and then had spent two months at the town house of a friend.

In hiding? No, he says; "I used to go out dancing at Castel's and Regine's every night."

And where is his share of the loot? That was not an admissible question.

Where does Spaggiari live now? "I've bought myself a three hundred and seventy-five-acre ranch in Argentina," he answered. "There's even a river with a twenty-seven-foot waterfall on my property. I'm happy in Argentina. It's a great country, with just about every European nationality represented. The mixture produces courage, strength, and friendliness."

Won't he be extradited? He shook his head. "Argentinian hospitality is something really unusual. Before anybody can be extradited, he has to go before a judge, who decides whether or not he deserves to be an Argentine citizen. But all that doesn't stop me from missing France. That's what I miss most of all."

Spaggiari smiled. The interview was at an end. "You'll be hearing about me before long," he said. "One way or another."